ART NOUVEAU
& ART DECO JEWELRY
An Identification & Value Guide

by

Lillian Baker

Photography by Dave Hammell

COLLECTOR BOOKS
P. O. Box 3009
Paducah, Kentucky 42001

For My Husband

Jewelry Displays on Plates & Cover:	Lillian Baker
***Art Nouveau* Jewelry Casket on**	
Cover:	Mildred Combs
* Jewelry Collections on Cover	Jenny Biddle
	Mildred Combs
	Lillian Baker
Art Deco Perfume Bottle on Cover:	Shirley's Antiques
Figurines & Accessories on Cover:	R. A. and L. Baker

*Jewelry pieces are shown on color plates.

The current values in this book should be used only as a guide. They are not intended to set prices, which vary from one section of the country to another. Auction prices as well as dealer prices vary greatly and are affected by condition as well as demand. Neither the Author nor the Publisher assumes responsibility for any losses that might be incurred as a result of consulting this guide.

Additional copies of this book may be ordered from:

COLLECTOR BOOKS
P. O. Box 3009
Paducah, Kentucky 42001
or
Lillian Baker
15237 Chanera Avenue
Alondra Park, Gardena, California 90249
@ $9.95 each, plus $1.00 postage & handling

Copyright: Lillian Baker, 1981
ISBN: 0-89145-158-7
This book or any part thereof may not be reproduced without the written consent of the Author and Publisher.

Printed by IMAGE GRAPHICS, Paducah, Kentucky

TABLE OF CONTENTS

"When to this natural magic of glinting metal and self-luminous stone is added the other magic of noble forms and colours artfully blended, we find ourselves in the presence of a genuine talisman . . ." ("Heaven and Hell", Aldous Huxley)

A NOTE FROM THE AUTHOR

A simplistic but hearty definition of Art Nouveau and Art Deco design is the triumph over functional line by artistic merit -- "Nature's random shapes . . . tamed by manual skill", (Graham Hughes). This is clearly shown in the succeeding pages of this textbook which looks to provide the missing handbook about "new art" jewelry.

Although there are dozens of reference works on the subject of Art Nouveau and Art Deco design and its influences, there is a woeful lack of singular reporting on that most important personal adornment -- JEWELRY. Therefore, this book attempts presenting the first textbook encompassing in distilled form, the diverse directions and paths that Art Nouveau and Art Deco periods stalked and shadowed.

Research into this period of Art Nouveau and Art Deco, presents a truly complex study with a transfer of many engaging theories from one author to another. The basis for many of the hypothesis set forth in their books are often suppositional or rather academic in nature. Some are even presumptive; a few rather impractical and abstract when one considers the available documentation and historical material in the archives.

Too many books about the Art Nouveau and Art Deco design eras tend to present historical reports of human endeavor in all areas, while ignoring what has been everlasting --the jewelry field. Here was personal adornment presented with as quakeful a jolt to mores and manners as the shuddering of change from cave-like existence to planetary landing.

The author, in presenting another concept covering the Art Nouveau and Art Deco periods, allows that there has been sufficient detailed reporting of the Aesthetic, Romantic, anti-Historical, and other "briefing" periods which lent change and strength and diversion to the "new art" of jewelry making. And in presenting a distilled version of this difficult and intransparent subject, the author in no way refutes the thesis and assumptions set forth by other writers, but rather attempts to intertexture the warf and woof of the fabric that represents the delicate mesh of Art Nouveau and Art Deco character, with all emphasis on JEWELRY.

The text seeks to provide new meaning to the work on this subject, but in a condensed and concrete form. It seeks to luminate a period of design which in itself bedazzles the reader and viewer alike. Its quest is to uncloud the obscure and to bring a new interest and concern for a luminescent period which was literally electrifying.

On a final note: "ART NOUVEAU & ART DECO JEWELRY", should be considered a supplement to the author's previous work, "ONE HUNDRED YEARS OF COLLECTIBLE JEWELRY (1850-1950)", published by Collector Books, (third printing, 1980); moreover, this newest study of the "new art" design, zeros in on the most neglected aspect of this all important period, the production of jewelry art in the nouveau and deco tradition.

"All art is at once surface and symbol . . .
those who read the symbol do so at their peril . . ."
(Oscar Wilde's "The Pictures of Dorian Gray")

SECTION I

**PEOPLE, PLACES, IDEAS, EVENTS
AND INSPIRATIONAL FORCES THAT
PROPELLED *ART NOUVEAU* &
ART DECO JEWELRY**

"A Fashion In Jewelry Should Last Longer Than A Fashion In Dresses Or In Hats . . . "(G. Mourey)

PEOPLE, PLACES, IDEAS, EVENTS and INSPIRATIONAL FORCES THAT PROPELLED *ART NOUVEAU* & ART DECO JEWELRY

The *new art* touched politics, society, religion, music, philosophy, ceramics, physics, chemistry, sculpture, poetry, literature, household objects, science, textiles, architecture (interior and exterior), furniture, the graphic arts, the written word, painted canvas, and the cinemas as well as fashions. "It", in turn, was affected by the changes in the above modes, materials, morals, and manners. But mostly by the politics, arts, and sciences of the end-of-a-century, "end of the world", gloom and doom: portents borne on the wings of war and a changing morality and social order. The "decadent" *fin' de siecle* period signaled the end of "the good old days", of "knowing one's place", realists vs. dreamers. An enlightened few saw the light of electricity as a benefit to mankind; others retreated, too shocked by its awesome and frightening potential, unable to cope with progress and blind to its beneficiary: "the masses".

A clear analogy today, as we face the end of the 20th Century, is in the challenges of the "new Space Age", the "Atomic Age", coming faster than light, faster than sound. In the sixties came the "aesthetics" — the Flower Children, those who looked back to "the distant drummer"; the Seventies brought somber reflections of "doom"; the Eighties seek refuge in "nostalgia" — antiques and collectibles of the decorative and decadent "new art" of circa 1875-1935.

In any event, the most radical effect of the "new art" was expressed in personal adornment: JEWELRY: *ART NOUVEAU* AND ART DECO.

NAMES TO RECKON WITH BECAUSE OF THEIR INFLUENCE IN THE DEVELOPMENT OF *ART NOUVEAU* AND ART DECO DESIGNS AND MOTIFS IN JEWELRY. (See THUMBNAIL SKETCHES for jewelers, designers, manufacturers, distributors, etc.)

Sculptors, painters, graphic artists, writers, etc., who influenced *Art Nouveau* designers and makers of jewelry: Klee, Whistler, Seurat*, Toulouse-Lautrec, Gauguin, Cézanne, Van Gogh, Troop, Walter Crane, Georges Lemmen, Aubrey Beardsley, Elbert Hubbard, Louis Icart*, Mondrian*, Dali*, Picasso*, Braque*, Calder*, Cocteau*, de Rivera*, Lipchitz, Chanel*, Schiaparelli*, Patou, Margaret de Patta (pioneer of "modern design"), Louis Sullivan, Candace Wheeler, and Mrs.E. Curtis Freschol, who designed the famed "Wisteria" Tiffany lamp. (* Denotes Art Deco influenced by Dadoism, Cubism and Surrealism, in their most abstract forms.) Coco Chanel was first to introduce "costume jewelry" in the Art Deco "mood". Chanel, Schiaparelli and Patou revolutionized fashions in dress and jewelry adornment.

NOUVEAU was "new", but lingered on the pessimism that came with the End-of-the-Century malaise — an affliction called "decadence". As Schmutzler wrote, *Art Nouveau* is "biological romanticism"; he might have added the word "immodest".

DECO was "young", optimistic, spirited, with a look to the "new century of progress", utilizing all that the machine could provide without sacrificing artistic merit.

Art Deco's vital designing came from the influence of electricity, exhibitionism, eclectism, eccentricity, and elite-ism . . . deco was to be a *decorative* piece of jewelry; *Art Nouveau*'s most memorable pieces are museum pieces, contrived for exhibitions and as artifacts to be *possessed* rather than to be worn. But it is the mass-produced manufacture of *Art Nouveau* jewelry copied from the French masters of "high" *Art Nouveau*, that enables collectors to enjoy and wear jewelry of the "new art" periods. And the media of synthetic materials adapted perfectly to the Art Deco *genre* of jewelry, and all "classes" could compete in fashion circles, adorned in assembly-line productions of fine Deco pieces.

DOMINANCE OF *SPEED* IN THE ART DECO FORM: ITS CAUSES AND PRELUDES

(1901) Marconi signaled across the Atlantic; (1902) The first radio message; (1903) Wireless communications accomplished between Great Britain and the United States; (1903) The Wright Brothers flew the first successful airplane at Kitty Hawk, North Carolina; (1909) Louis Bleriot flew across the English Channel; (1912) R.C. Fowler made the first transcontinental airplane flight, Jacksonville (Florida) to San Francisco (California); (1913) Parcel Post established, leading to the large mail-order catalogue business that brought "Paris fashions" in "new art" jewelry on a mass-production basis, to the "common folk"; (1922) Radio enters the homes of millions and the world becomes seemingly smaller and less remote. The newly formed "tabloids" exploit "bathing beauties" and headlines the changing mores: "flaming youths and reckless maidens" who take to parked cars; "gin, cigarettes, rolled stockings, lipstick, rouge, night clubs, petting parties . . . gate-crashing . . . saxophones, sex magazines, motion pictures — and Freud". In 1924, came the "shocking" news that "girls (are) allowed to smoke at Bryn Mawr"; (1927) Lindbergh's flight across the Atlantic and the "speed" motif of Art Deco design crosses all boundaries of imaginative abstraction.

Christopher Dresser, botanist, influenced American *Art Nouveau* design. "True ornamentation is of purely mental origin and consists of symbolised imagination or emotion only." He believed there was "nothing too mundane to be transformed into a thing of beauty", if it was from nature.

Gabriel Mourey, (circa 1901), wrote of the *nouveau* jewelry: "Remain they certainly will, to bear witness to the audacious fancy, the creative faculty of the artists, and as a sort of passionate homage laid by the men of today at the feet of the Eternal Feminine . . . "

Graham Hughes, ("Modern Jewelry"), " . . . The best jewels are the most im-

7

aginative,the most individual, the most diverse in inspiration. They are not always the most sensitive. Sensitivity is no substitute for the creative urge, and new jewels showing the most commendable and vigorous style are often not the most sensitive. Sensitivity often means mediocrity; directness may mean genius."

Linda Campbell Franklin, ("Antiques and Collectibles"), The Arts and Crafts Movement was "partly based on the erroneous idea that handiwork is intrinsically more valuable than machine work." The "new art" jewelry abstractions harnessed the "applied arts" and became the main innovators of design for machine and jewelry "for the masses". Thus, "fine" and 'applied" art combined to present variations in personal adornment that was to please many and raise protests in a few like William Morris who said that "the great intangible machine of commercial tyranny which oppress us all" would bring "calamities". In the end, it was more prudent to design for those defiant machine-monsters, to make them eat out of man's hand and not be devoured in the taming.

Dante Gabriel Rossetti, (1828-1882) English poet and painter was the driving force of the Pre-Raphaelite's; exponent of the Renaissance conception of "human nobility"; leader who followed in the footsteps of English painter, Sir Edward Coley Burne-Jones, painting classical, religious, medieval and symbolic scenes filled with mysticism and "romanticism". The Aesthetic Period of the "new art" was much influenced by the paintings and writings of the "romanticists", and jewelry designers copied motifs expressed in the other arts. The Aesthetic Period jewelry shows fine figurative work, whereas Art Deco is strictly non-figurative. Other "romanticists": John Ruskin, Elizabeth & Robert Browning, Lord Alfred Tennyson.

John Ruskin, proponent of the "aesthetic craze", wrote that "The loveliest things are the least useful — lilies and peacock feathers . . .". These lovely motifs advanced upon the *nouveau* scene, leaving the "medievals" behind.

James MacKay, in "*Turn of the Century Antiques*", wrote that "The Arts and Crafts Movement is often regarded as the epitome of inspired amateurism, wrapped in a nostalgia for a medieval ideal which never existed." Nevertheless, it was the catalyst for bringing a new consciousness of beauty in "lilies and peacocks".

Oscar Wilde started the vogue of "art for art's sake", and he brought strength to the "aesthetic" craze which swept England, France, and America. He favored carrying a lily or a sunflower, and designers of "aesthetic" jewelry chose these flowers which lent themselves to high *repousse* work in brooches and pendants. When the "Edwardian dandies" disappeared, enter the giants of the cosmopolitan age: Diaghilev, Picasso, Stravinsky, Cocteau, Copeland, Curie, Darwin, Debussy, Edison, Einstein, T.S. Eliot, Henry Ford, Freud, and Gandhi — major influences in the arts and politics which shaped fashion and decorative ornamentation — jewelry of the "new art" era.

Charles Ives, (1874-1954), the American composer, was opposed to the concept of "art for art's sake". He said it was a corruption of ideals, and that a true and complete artist requires "spiritual sturdiness", a requirement completely lacking in the decadentness of the *nouveau* artist/jeweler.

Thomas Cook began his "Cook's Tour" (1841), followed in 1912 by the American Express world travel offerings to appease mass appetites. The Duke of Wellington objected to the early railways for "all social classes" because this form of travel would encourage "the lower classes to move about".

(1835) Great Britain established its Government Schools of Design to encourage advancement and upgrading of industrial design, which eventually affected mass-produced jewelry for the "*nouveau*" rich and the "working classes".

(1851) Great Britain's "Crystal Palace Exhibition", with its introduction into the "Machine Age" and the miracle of *Electricity*. The machine and electricity made possible electro-plating — gilded varieties of metals for jewelry, machine-stamped for mass production.

(1854) London's Watercolour Society held its first showing of Oriental arts which greatly affected the "new arts" in jewelry design and execution.

(1860) Discovery of the Comstock Silver Lode, Nevada, largest in America. Silver was a less expensive source of suitable metal for *nouveau* and deco jewelry. It was the preferred metal for Arts & Crafts jewelers, especially in Germany and Scandinavia; American machine-made, mass-produced, "*nouveau* jewelry *ala Paris*" relied heavily on silver, i.e., manufacturers: Unger Bros., Gorham, Kerr, etc.

(1861) Socialist, William Morris, founded Morris & Co., (England), closing its doors in 1940. Morris was the "voice" of the British Arts & Crafts Movement, but mainly in the execution of furniture and textiles. Jewelry design and production was still off-stage waiting for Liberty & Co. to give it impetus when it came on cue in 1875.

(1862) Britain's Mary Eliza Haweis, (1848-1898), was forerunner of the "Bohemian" sect that advocated return to Medieval "simplicity" in dress and jewelry. Wearing a loose, unhindered, unbelted frock, enhanced by strings of beads, she was identified with the Aesthetic movement — the "flower children" of the 1860's.

(1862) *Porte Chinoise*, Paris, held first Oriental art boutique. Not to be outdone, London featured the first Japanese art and wares exhibit in the International Exhibit Hall. Both exhibitions had a dynamic affect on "new art" jewelry design.

(1868) American graphic artist, William H. (Will) Bradley made a splash on the scene dominated by Britain's Aubrey Beardsley. Both men produced inspirational designs for *Art Nouveau* jewelry.

(1870) Great Britain's "Aesthetic Movement" begins and extends through 1890. Strongest influences: Aubrey Beardsley (graphics); Oscar Wilde (writer/lecturer); James McNeill Whistler (American painter) — all under the spell of Japanese art and design.

9

(1871) The Guild of St. George founded in England.

(1872) Vincent Aubrey Beardsley (Aubrey Beardsley), Britain's major graphic artist continues to influence art and jewelry design in Britain, the Continent, and America. Influenced by Whistler, Beardsley had turned toward Japonism, and became more popular than ever. His great productivity period was from 1872-1898. In 1872, London's International Exhibition showed Indian jewelry from India, and between the Oriental and Indian designs, the upswing of eclectic patterns in jewelry was taking hold.

(1874) At age 40, William Morris begins his experiments with fabric design. Morris had already softened toward machine-made products "for the masses", although he continued to produce merchandise for the "elite" — the only society that could afford his hand-made individually crafted items.

(1875) Britain's Liberty & Company, London, was founded on the basis of pro-moting Arts and Crafts designs, but more particularly of the Glasgow School of Celtic motifs. The jewelry designers/artists were in strict anonymity for at that time Britain allowed manufacturing/retailers to mark their own trade-mark on merchan-dise. Arthur Lasenby Liberty, founder of Liberty & Company, was a major force in promoting the "new art for the masses" in Great Britain, Europe, Scandinavia, America, and in Scotland. Some of the foremost designers of England and Glasgow worked for Liberty. (See Thumbnail Sketches)

(1876) Philadelphia Centennial Exposition, with its Oriental displays of art works featuring Sunflower and Lotus motifs, influenced American designs for "new art" jewelry.

(1876) Queen Victoria is heralded Empress of India, and Indian jewelry became fashionable as well as a source of design for the eclectic pieces of "new art" jewelry.

(1879) Louis Comfort Tiffany opens his American Workshop Studio where he and his associates produce pieces greatly influenced by Japanese two-dimensional graphic art, as well as the British Arts & Crafts Movement which had crossed the seas to America. Tiffany's Workshop Studio left its permanent mark on the *Art Nouveau* period.

(1881) *L'Art Moderne* review is founded by Octave Maus in Brussels, enhancing the effect Belgium's *nouveau* jewelry had on German-speaking countries.

(1882) Great Britain's Oscar Wilde, having gained a strong foothold and bold reputation, makes an 18-month tour of America, advocating his "aesthetic ideals". His audiences were bands of idealists and dreamers, like minstrels of old.

(1882) Englishman, Arthur Heygate Mackmurdo, produces exceptional tapestry designs adapted by German and French jewelry designers. It is this year that The Century Guild is founded, one of many such Guilds to bear influence on the "new art".

10

(1883) William Morris becomes spokesman for the Arts and Crafts Exhibition Society.

(1884) Brussels' *Les Vignet*, (The Twenty), form a studio for Belguim's *art nouveau* under the prime leadership of Victor Horta (designer) and Philippe Wolfers (jeweler). And in London, *avante garde* artists sweep into the Industrial Arts of India Exhibition, while another influence is born: England's Keswick School of Industrial Art. "Art for art's sake" is becoming "art for industry's sake". Aiding this premise is The Art and Workers' Guild (England).

(1885) The American Art Workers Guild is inaugurated at Providence, R.I., soon to become a leading jewelry manufacturing city. The Art Workers Guild is simultaneously formed in Great Britain.

(1886) William Morris and Walter Crane are leaders in the formation of the Arts & Crafts Exhibition Society, where sources of design are incorporated into jewelry.

(1887) Yet another British guild: The Guild of Handicraft.

(1888) Britain's T. Cobden Sanderson (AKA T.J. Cobden), is credited with changing "The Combined Art Society" name, (adopted by William Morris and his followers), to the more acceptable "Arts & Crafts Society", whose aim was to retain a sense of artistry in the "traditional skills". The final name adopted: "Arts and Crafts Exhibition Society".

(1889) *Exposition Universelle*, Paris, with its Eiffel Tower, brings together many designers whose work reflects the *fin' de siecle* decadence intruding quickly into the last decade of the 19th Century. The "high" *Art Nouveau* jewelry pedestal awaits the crowning "glories" of the forthcoming 1900 Exposition. Britain's Home Arts and Industries Association flourishes, as Victorian "parlor-work" excels.

(1890) England's Birmingham Guild of Handicraft is founded, and some of the finest designers and jewelers will make Birmingham the main manufacturing center of fine jewelry for the masses.

(1890) Dutchman, Jan Toorop (1858-1928), dominates the nineties as a designer with great influence in the Netherland's school of symbolist painters, who are inspiration for jewelry designs in Brussels. Walter Crane's graphics still dominates the field in England, and especially at the Bromsgrove Guild of Applied Art. In Birmingham, the Vittoria Street School for Jewelers & Silversmiths fortifies Birmingham's position in jewelry manufacture; at its heels is the Yattendon Metalworking Class doing copper work for Liberty & Company.

(1891) Walter Crane tours America and his graphics/illustrations win popular approval and influence jewelry design.

(1892) Belgium's Victor Horta, architect, becomes a highly influential source of Brussel's *avante garde* artists, some of whom design *nouveau* jewelry.

(1893) French graphic artist, Jules Cheret, makes his popular lithographed poster of Löie Fuller, whose dance "partner" was the new toy -- electricity. She danced while colored lights flirted with gossamer veils, transforming Loie into "the butterfly lady". She was the inspiration for several "high" *art nouveau* pieces of jewelry, which were then copied for manufacture in America. Fuller's protege was Isadora Duncan whose politics -- rather than her talent -- have kept her name in the limelight. Meanwhile, at the Chicago World's Fair, American *art nouveau* was the star of that show, even while Frank Lloyd Wright cried for more symmetry and the April issue of *"The Studio"* magazine propagandized for simpler themes with artistic merit in the American Arts & Craft Movement.

(1894) Antwerp held its International Exhibition, and between this and the 1893 World's Columbian Exposition, (Chicago World's Fair), a marvelous change was to take place in the following year (1895).

(1895) Following his visit to the Chicago World's Fair, Samuel Bing opened his *"Galleries de l'Art Nouveau"*. It became the showplace for "modern" designers and jewelers, and attracted international acclaim. It was here that René Lalique designed and executed his first brooch featuring a nude female. This became his "trademark" which was soon pirated by other jewelry designers and makers. In this same year, The Minneapolis Arts and Crafts Society was a force to be reckoned with in the "new art", even though newly founded.

(1896) America's first issue of *House Beautiful* was published, (December), with articles and designs by England's Morris, Crane, Ashbee, and Voysey -- all influencing fashion trends and jewelry.
William Morris, noted force behind the Arts and Crafts Movement, begun in Great Britain, dies after compromising his "aims" to the Mother-of-Invention: machinery, mass-production, electricity, and "art for industry".

(1897) Boston forms its Arts and Crafts Society and Brussels holds its International Exhibit; then Chicago broadens its scope with the formation of the Chicago Arts and Crafts Society. But dominating the movement of "new art" abroad, was the Dresden Exhibition, (Germany), which powered the founding of the "modern movement" by the *avant garde* artists in the flourishing colonies of Munich, Darmstadt, Dresden, and Schenebek. The Munich Workshop was the real beginning of the *art nouveau* in Germany known as "Jugendstil", (young art).

(1898) Vienna's first *Secession* Exhibition -- influenced in its jewelry forms by the Glasgow School of design. At this time, C. R. Ashbee, noted British jeweler/designer exhibited in Chicago and was accorded a bravo reception.

(1899) Darmstadt, Germany: artist's colony founded on fertile soil of *art nouveau* innovators in the Glasgow School style of jewelry design.

(1900) *L'Exposition Universelle* on the *Champ de Mars*, Paris, where *art nouveau* reached its peak of perfection in its unrivalled showcase provided by the master jeweler, René Lalique. At this exhibition, Löie Fuller, Isadora Duncan, Jean

Lorrain and Cléo de Mérode, were principal dance attractions. The latter, a classical dancer with a "perfect oval face", was the model for mermaids, fairies, and other legendary winsome maidens for *nouveau* jewelry designs. Fuller's veils became butterfly wings, and she was called "Butterfly Woman" along with American dancer, Jean Lorrain, both of whom are depicted on *nouveau* jewelry and other souvenir artifacts of the 1900 exhibition.

(1901) Following the impressive, potent, and inspiring Paris Exhibition (1900), England's Artificers' Guild was formed and Glasgow held its International Exhibit showing the infiltration of ideas acquired from that experience and exposure to the "new art" which resulted in a drive to compete with less "decadent" designs of France and Belgium.

(1901) Gustav Stickley, Syracuse (N. Y.), influenced by his visit abroad where he met Ashbee, Voysey, and S. Bing, publishes his first edition of "*The Craftsman*" which advocates the less provocative and "decadent" Arts & Crafts Movement advocated by William Morris and his followers. As the "high" *Art Nouveau* jewelry designs were being reproduced as "Parisian" fashion for "American tastes" and literally flooding jewelry catalogues and showcases, Stickley became alarmed and wrote in the 1904 issue of "*The Craftsman*", that *Art Nouveau* was "wilful and somewhat dangerous", and added, "...non-structural objects, those whose forms present a chaos of lines which the eye can follow only lazily or hopelessly, should be swept out from the dwellings of the people, since, in the mental world, they are the same volcanoes or earthquakes in the world of matter. They are the creators of disorder and destruction. The shapes of things...should carry ideas of stability and symmetry...".

(1902) Ashbee exhibits at the 15th Vienna *Secession* Exhibition, and Van de Velde opens his Craft School in Weimar leading to the founding of the German *Bauhaus* in 1919. The latter was a tremendous force in the Art Deco movement.

(1902) Edgar Simpson, influenced by Ashbee's work, exhibits in Vienna *Secessionist* exhibition.

(1903) Josef Hoffman and Koloman Moser found the *Wiener Werkstatte*, (Vienna Workshop) which was the culminating force of the *Sezession* (or *Secession*) Movement in Austria which was highly influenced by the Glasgow School, and particularly by the "Glasgow Four". (See GLOSSARY)

(1907) Japanese artist, Sugawara, shares his secrets of lacquer techniques and crafts with Jean Dunand in Paris workshop. (Dunand executed lacquer panels in French luxury liner "Normandie" in top-notch Art Deco form, 1935.) Katsu Shamanaka was a student of Sugawara, and worked with Maurice Dufréne, jewelry designer. These lacquer techniques were used in Art Deco period.

(1908) Louis Icart's first cover (Dec. 1908) appears on *La Critique Theatrale;* graphics by Icart depict Art Deco's 1920-1930 passion for Parisiennes and obsession with speed.

13

(1908) Two giants meet: Frank Lloyd Wright and C. R. Ashbee, both highly influential designers. Ashbee's influence is in the Arts & Crafts Movement of the "new art"; Wright's leans toward development of a further aim to "create a new beauty from apparent ugliness", and insists that beauty must come from the *use* of man's machines. Ashbee reportedly thought Wright's designs were "too bizarre" and "away from all traditional beauty", and America's farsighted and gifted architect, Wright, found Ashbee's "squares and geometric lines...fussy and restless." The next year, (1909), would bring more weight to Wright's plea for change and his call for clemency toward "*what the machine has wrought*".

(1909) The Russian Ballet shocks Paris with its technicolor production of "She'he'razade." A new trend in color and line appear in subsequent fashion plates by Georges Lepape, Georges Barbier and fashion illustrator, Erte'. The colors are shades of the transitionary trends of the "new art" from *nouveau* to Deco boldness.

(1911) Glasgow's International Exhibit, still a force to be reckoned with in the field of jewelry.

(1913) England's Omega Workshops formed, with influential designers finding a showcase for their work.

(1922) Egyptian motifs abound with the opening of Tutankhamen's tomb, and become even more prevalent in the subsequent years leading to the 1925 Paris Exhibition from which "Art Deco" gets its name.

(1925) *L' Exposition Internationale des Arts Decoratifs et Industriels Modernes* gives the name "Art Deco" to history of decorative arts. The Paris exhibition to "unite art with industry" and to exclude "all copies and imitations of ancient styles", did not preclude using ancient subjects as long as they were shown in "modern stylization". Exhibiting Art Deco jewelers: Paul Brandt, Jean Fouquet, Georges Fouquet, Eric Gragge, A. Leveille, Yolande Mas, Raymond Templier, and Gerard Sandoz. Eclectic designs included Moorish, Egyptian, Asian, African and Persian influences.

As early as the 16th Century, Dürer wrote, "Art is hidden in nature". The "new art", centuries later, became his object lesson.

Chikamatsu, Japanese playwright, defined art as "something lifted from the real by stylization." Furthermore, he emphasized that "art is something which lies in the slender margin between the real and the unreal." M. Chikamatsu, (1736-1795) has provided an apt definition of "new art" jewelry concepts, for although the jewelry of the *nouveau* period may appear as mere innovation, careful analysis reveals a potent originality expressing a true art form.

SECTION II

COLOR PLATES & DESCRIPTIONS
1 through 50

The jewelry pictured on the color plates within the pages of this book, represent *art nouveau* and art deco pieces in private collections and those available for sale at prices within the reach of both novice and connoisseur. The jewelry pieces have never before been shown in any previous book or publication, and although many pieces are of museum quality they represent types of "new art" jewelry available to the reader/collector.

PLATE 1.

Top:

BELT BUCKLE, 2/pc. *Art Nouveau.* 4¼"x2½" wingspread, w/six peacock-eye glass sets, cabachon cut, bezel-mounted. (See PLATE 23 for open view mechanism of unique clasp). The butterfly is a Chinese symbol of joy and wedded bliss.

Center:

DECORATIVE ORNAMENT, Art Deco. Buckle-type scarab ornament, for turban or cummerbund, w/four sew-holes. 6½" wingspread, 3½" vertical measurement. Carved and molded plastic.

Bottom:

BROOCH, *Art Nouveau.* Silver brooch, originally conceived as a belt buckle which was converted with c.1900 jeweler's findings. Large 4"x2½" brooch w/floral motif of chased and embossed "Lunaria" --Satinpods, or sometimes called Honesty Plant. (Aesthetic Period motif) (Mildred Combs Collection)

17

PLATE 2.

Row 1, Center: BROOCH, Art Deco, plastic imitation amber and jet. Phoenix bird wings with black scarab. Egyptian influence. (Author's Collection)

Row 2, Center: BROOCH, Art Deco, gilt over brass w/carved carnelian. (Jenny Biddle Collection)

Row 3, Left: BROOCH, Art Deco, oxidized brass w/*faux* gemstone. (Jenny Biddle Collection)

Row 3, Right: BROOCH, Art Deco, oxidized brass w/green and amethyst color glass stones. (Jenny Biddle Collection)

Row 4, Left to Right: HATPIN, *Art Nouveau,* gilt over brass w/enamel. (Author's Collection)

HATPIN, Art Deco, plastic w/brass contrived scarab, accented w/insert of a plastic molded pharoh. (Author's Collection)

NECKLACE, Art Deco, Bakelite beads and pendant; plastic w/brass, Egyptian symbols. (Author's Collection)

PR. HATPINS, *Art Nouveau, faux* tortoise, w/metallic gilt over brass ornamentation. (Sylvia & Stan Katz Collection)

PLATE 3.

Row 1:   BROOCH, *Art Nouveau*, Bat in cultist stance, *plique-a-jour* enamel on marked sterling.

Row 2:   PENDANT, *Art Nouveau, plique-a-jour* and painted enamel on sterling, w/gold wash. 2 pc. pendant, slides apart to reveal small mirror. Artist's mark. (French)

Row 3, Left: BROOCH, *Art Nouveau*, sterling w/gold wash. Unger Bros., Newark, N.J.

Row 3, Right: PIN W/WATCH HOOK, *Art Nouveau*, sterling w/gold wash. Small hook on reverse side accommodates watch.

Row 4:   BROOCH, *Art Nouveau*, half oyster shell design to display pearl; sterling w/gold wash.

Row 5:   PENDANT W/CHAIN, *Art Nouveau*, Theodore Fahrner (German), *plique-a-jour* enamel on sterling. Note unusual safety clasp and hand wrought link chain.
(Papillion [Sherman Oaks] Collection;
Mike Iorge & Martin Wolpert Collection)

PLATE 4.

Top: BROOCH, *Art Nouveau*, marked: Sterling. *basse-taille* and *Champleve* enameling.

Center: BROOCH, *Art Nouveau, basse-taille* enamel, hallmarked: Sterling, (Sheffield 1904)

Bottom: BROOCH, *Art Nouveau, basse-taille* enamel. Arts and Crafts influence.
(Mildred Combs Collection)

PLATE 5.

Top: NECKLACES, Art Deco. Three Czechoslovakian necklaces of molded glass. Egyptian motifs: mummy, scarab and pharohs. (Circa 1920)

Center: EARRINGS, Art Deco, gilt over brass, wire work set w/Czech. molded glass.

Bottom: NECKLACE, Art Deco, w/Mayan and Egyptian design influence. Green enameling and *faux* jade in German silver mounts.
(Mildred Combs Collection)

PLATE 6.

Left to Right: PENDANT, *Art Nouveau*, 14 carat, Four Leaf Clover w/3" diameter. Green *plique-a-jour* enameling.

PENDANT W/CHAIN, *Art Nouveau*, 14 carat, w/approx. 1½" wingspread. Three shades *plique-a-jour* enamel, w/¼" *baroque* pearl drop and one diamond.

PENDANT W/CHAIN, *Art Nouveau*, 14 carat, w/*baroque* pearl drop. 2½" overall, w/1-1/8" wingspread. Green *plique-a-jour* enamel. No gem accents.
(Jenny Biddle Collection/Cape Cottage Antiques.)

PLATE 7.

Top
Left to Right: RING, *Art Nouveau*, 14K, uncommon full-face woman, fine *repousse* work accented w/1 diamond and 2 rubies. Entire girdle of ring is engraved w/Forget-Me-Not flowers.

RING, *Art Nouveau*, 14K, carved ivory profile adorned in winged headdress of Mercury, god of commerce and gain, also symbolic of a certain fickleness in nature. One diamond accent.

RING, *Art Nouveau*, 14K, woman's profile w/3 diamonds in hair, and catching another diamond in long tendril of her tresses.

Bottom
Left to Right: RING, *Art Nouveau*, 14K, coin-shape, w/woman's profile in bold relief, accented by diamond at throat.

RING, *Art Nouveau,* 14K, woman's profile executed in white, pink, and Roman gold.

RING, *Art Nouveau*, 14K very heavy mounting, w/woman's hair performing as design factor on complete circlet of ring which is highlighted by one diamond and one sapphire.
(Jenny Biddle Collection/Cape Cottage Antiques)

PLATE 8.

Top: BELT BUCKLE, Art Deco, white alloy frame, *pavé* set
                rhinestones. Simulated hasp.

Center: PURSE FRAME, Art Deco, heavy sterling frame set
                w/garnets and marcasites. Black glass turban-type clasp.
                (German)

Bottom: STUD BUTTONS, Art Deco, trio of lady's stud buttons,
                (shown obverse and reverse). Popular harlequin mask of
                Deco period. Pierced mold, German silver, *pavé* set
                rhinestones.
                (Mildred Combs Collection)

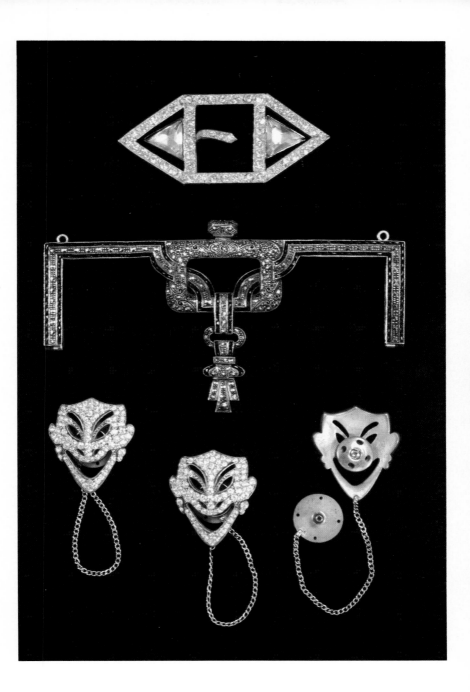

PLATE 9.

Left to Right: NECKLACE, Art Deco (transitional). Czechoslovakian glass imitation cabachon cut jade w/foil backed faceted rhinestones. *Secession* Period.

NECKLACE, Art Deco (transitional). Pink foiled glass; marked "Czechoslovakia", w/enamel and filigree drops. (Prior to 1925 *Arts Decoratifs* exhibit)

NECKLACE, Art Deco (transitional). Peking glass. Chinese "goldfish" or "carp" beads w/sterling silver separators that suggest Oriental ideographs. (Mildred Combs Collection)

PLATE 10.

Row 1, Left: BROOCH, *Art Nouveau,* sterling, Byzantine design by Mucha. (French)

Center: PENDANT w/chain, *Art Nouveau,* sterling. Unger Bros., Newark, N.J.

Right: BROOCH, *Art Nouveau,* sterling, Unger Bros., Newark, N.J. (French influence)

Row 2, Left: BROOCH, *Art Nouveau,* pierced sterling front w/star punch mark on back. (From a French design)

Center: BROOCH, *Art Nouveau,* sterling front w/star punch mark on reverse side. (American)

Right: LOCKET, *Art Nouveau,* sterling w/clover mark. (Clover was Dublin's assay mark for imported silver, 1904-06)

Row 3, Left: BROOCH, *Art Nouveau.* Sterling, unmarked maker.

Center: BROOCH, *Art Nouveau,* exceptionally large sterling brooch, w/high *repousse* work and detailed chasing and embossing, w/pierce work.

Right: WATCH HOLDER, *Art Nouveau,* sterling, *repousse* work w/hook on reverse to hang watch. Star punch mark.

Row 4, Left: BROOCH, *Art Nouveau,* sterling w/star punch mark.

Center: BROOCH, *Art Nouveau,* unique piece depicting female violinist w/ingenious pierce work, embossing and *repousse.* Sterling w/star punch mark.

Right: BROOCH, *Art Nouveau,* sterling, open work, high *repousse,* w/star punch mark.
(Papillion [Sherman Oaks]; Mike Iorg & Martin Wolpert Collection)

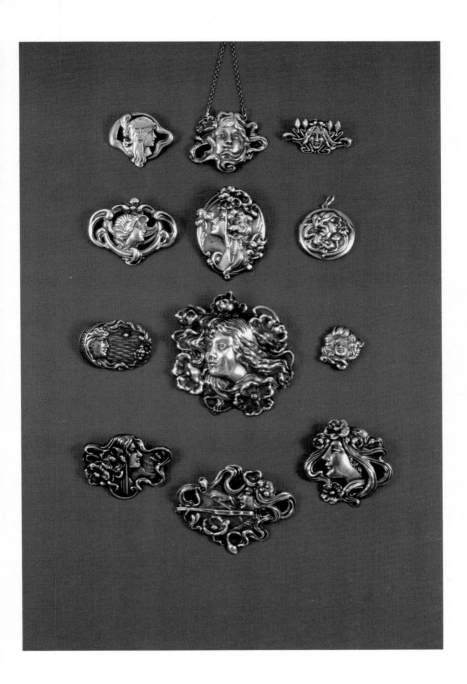

33

PLATE 11.

Row 1, Left: PENDANT w/chain, *Art Nouveau*, 14K, *plique-a-jour* enamel w/¾ profile of woman with sweeping tendrils of hair. (French)
(B. Halskov & Shelby Lewis Collection)

Center: PENDANT w/chain, *Art Nouveau*, heart-shaped 14K, *plique-a-jour* enamel.
(B. Halskov & Shelby Lewis Collection)

Right: BRACELET, *Art Nouveau*, gold over sterling, lapis-blue molded glass center stones, w/*plique-a-jour* enamel triangular designs. (*Jugendstil*) Marked: W.M.C.
(Mildred Combs Collection)

Row 2, Left: PENDANT, *Art Nouveau*, 14K, mauve-color *plique-a-jour*, poppy design w/diamond.
(B. Halskov & Shelby Lewis Collection)

Center: PENDANT, *Art Nouveau*, 14K, full-face woman, *plique-a-jour* enamel w/pearl drop, 6 diamonds, one sapphire.
(B. Halskov & Shelby Lewis Collection)

Bottom, Left: HATPINS, three, *Art Nouveau*; sterling, *plique-a-jour* w/two *baroque* pearls.
(Mildred Combs Collection)
Sterling w/amethyst & marcasites; sterling w/chrysoprase & marcasites. Marked: *Depose*. (French)
(Author's Collection)

Center: BROOCH, *Art Nouveau*, sterling dragonfly, *plique-a-jour* enamel. French. (Author's Collection)

Lower Right: PENDANT, *Art Nouveau*, small 14K, daffodil design, *plique-a-jour* enamel w/diamond and *baroque* pearl drop.
(B. Halskov & Shelby Lewis Collection)

PLATE 12.

HATPIN, *Art Nouveau*, 2¼" hinged scarab, gilt over brass, on 10" pin-shank. Scarab enhanced with *pate-de-verre* glass insert. Unique piece. (See Glossary)

PENDANT, *Art Nouveau*, 2½" *pate-de-verre* glass. On obverse side, in mold: "HB" stylized initials form head of ram or sheep, and "A. Walter Mfg." (Henri Berge) (Mildred Combs Collection)

PLATE 13.

Left to Right:

PENDANT W/CHAIN, *Art Nouveau*, 14 carat, floral *plique-a-jour* w/*baroque* pearl.

PENDANT WITHOUT CHAIN, *Art Nouveau*, 14 carat, w/varigated colours of *plique-a-jour* enamel. *Champleve* enameled Tulip. Piece is highlighted by 5 diamonds.

PENDANT W/CHAIN, *Art Nouveau*, 14K, floral w/diamond stamen and *baroque* pearl drop. *Plique-a-jour* enamel.
(Jenny Biddle Collection/Cape Cottage Antiques)

PLATE 14.

Row 1:   BROOCH, *Art Nouveau. Champleve* and *basse-taille* enamel, *vermeil.*

Row 2:   BROOCH, *Art Nouveau.* Flying fish motif in *champleve* and *basse-taille* enamel. (A pair of fish is the Chinese symbol for marriage and a charm against evil.)

Row 3:   *LAVALIERE, Art Nouveau.* Rare Venetian glass mosaic work in gilded and hand-wrought silver. (Celtic design, Glasgow School)

Row 4:   BUCKLE, 2/pc., *Art Nouveau, champleve* and *basse-taille* enamels. Sterling.
(Mildred Combs Collection)

PLATE 15.

Left: HATPIN, *Art Nouveau*,gilt on brass w/simulated topaz, Egyptian motif.

Top Right: PR. POMPADOUR COMBS, *Art Nouveau, faux* tortoise w/gilt brass and turquoise glass accents.

Bottom Right: BACK COMB, *Art Nouveau,* tortoise w/gilt brass and turquoise glass accents.
(Mildred Combs Collection)

PLATE 16.

EARRINGS, *Art Nouveau*, 14K w/bezel-set opals. 1" x 1-1/8" ear-bobs on 1" wire.
(Jenny Biddle Collection/Cape Cottage Antiques)

PLATE 17.

Left to Right: RING, *Art Nouveau*, 14 carat, w/1" circumference, highly engraved and pierced. Hair is accented w/diamond and rubies.

PENDANT W/CHAIN, *Art Nouveau*, 14 carat, 1-¾" overall, w/fresh-water *baroque* pearl. A ruby rosette adorns hair. Aesthetic and "romantic" influence. ". . .Long let me bite your heavy black tresses.When I gnaw your elastic and rebellious hair, it seems that I am eating memories." Charles Baudelaire, French poet, (1821-1867)
(Jenny Biddle Collection/Cape Cottage Antiques)

43

PLATE 18.

Top: BROOCH or pr. of dress clips (convertible), Art Deco, w/*pavé* set green glass stones and foil-backed brilliants. White Alloy.

Center: BROOCH, Art Deco, abstract stylized Chinese *Chou* design. White alloy, set w/rhinestones.

Bottom: BROOCH, Art Deco, highly stylized winged and helmeted Hermes, speedy messenger of the gods,depicted in dynamic fantasy of rhinestones set into white alloy.
(Mildred Combs Collection)

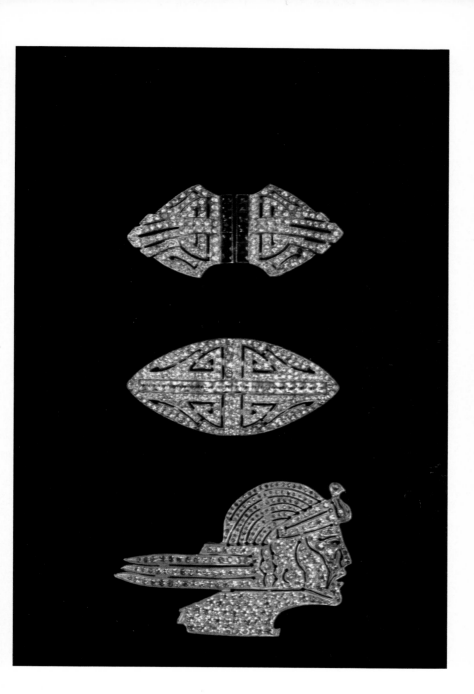

PLATE 19.

Row 1, Top: PENDANT w/chain, Art Deco, sterling set w/chrysoprase and marcasites.

Center: NECKLACE, Art Deco, sterling set w/chrysoprase and marcasites.

Bottom: NECKLACE, Art Deco, sterling set w/chrysoprase and marcasites.

Row 2, Left: DRESS CLIP, Art Deco, marcasites & sterling.

Center: PENDANT, Art Deco, carved carnelian set in sterling w/marcasites.

Right: BROOCH, Art Deco, sterling set w/marcasites.

Row 3: BRACELET, Art Deco, sterling set w/chrysoprase and marcasites.

Row 4: BRACELET, Art Deco, heavy sterling w/marcasites.

Row 5, Left: EARRINGS w/posts, Art Deco, sterling w/marcasites.

Center: *LAVALIERE*, Art Deco, sterling set with sodalite gemstones, accented w/marcasites.

Right: EARRINGS w/clips, Art Deco, sterling w/marcasites. (Jenny Biddle Collection/Cape Cottage Antiques)

PLATE 20.

Row 1:   PENDANT w/chain, *Art Nouveau*, hallmarked: Charles Horner. Enamel on sterling. (Arts & Crafts influence) (Mildred Combs Collection)

Row 2:   2/pc. BUCKLE, *Art Nouveau*, approx. 4½" across. Unusually heavy buckle, hallmarked: sterling, (London, 1901), signed by unidentified maker: Hss-LD. 20-84. (Aesthetic Period influence) (Jenny Biddle Collection/Cape Cottage Antiques)

Row 3:   BROOCH *Art Nouveau*, hallmarked: Charles Horner. Thistle motif, (Celtic), sterling. (Author's Collection)

Row 4, Left: HATPIN, *Art Nouveau*, hallmarked: Charles Horner, sterling, Thistle motif.

Center: HATPIN, *Art Nouveau*, oxidized silver Lotus (Water Lily), set w/*faux* diamond and ruby. Lotus flower is the Chinese symbol of creative power, purity, and feminine genius.The pod symbolizes the blessings of offspring.

Right: HATPIN, *Art Nouveau*, Charles Horner, hallmarked English sterling w/topaz color glass Thistle design. (Three hatpins are from author's collection)

49

PLATE 21.

Top: BRACELET, Art Deco, German silver set w/Czechoslovakian molded glass. Egyptian motifs: pharoh and scarab, the latter being the symbol of the sun.

Center: BRACELET, Art Deco, copper over brass mounting, set w/identically designed and molded Czech. glass in varied shades.

Bottom: EARRINGS w/clips, Art Deco, oxidized metal engraved clips w/2" drop earrings.Czechoslovakian molded glass, depicting Egyptian God, Osiris. According to legend, the falcon fanned new life into this oldest of the gods. Falcon's wings are a common motif in Egyptian design which influenced both *Art Nouveau* and Art Deco artists. (Mildred Combs Collection)

PLATE 22.

PENDANT W/CHAIN, *Art Nouveau*, 14K, green and lavendar effused *plique-a-jour* enameled 2¼" long pendant, 1¼" wide. One center diamond w/2 opals. Rare chain of linked *plique-a-jour* enamel intervals. (High *Art Nouveau* Period)
(Jenny Biddle Collection/Cape Cottage Antiques)

51

PLATE 23.

Row 1, Top: BUCKLE, *Art Nouveau*. Hat-band or waist-band buckle w/utilitarian safety pin for attaching cockade of feathers or bouquet of flowers. (Pat. May 6, 1905)

Row 2, Left: SCARF HOLDER, (slide), *Art Nouveau*. Silver w/gilt. Stickpin device on reverse side to prevent slippage.

Right: CROSS, *Art Nouveau*. German silver w/chasing and engraving. (Aesthetic Period)

Row 3:   PINS, set of 3, *Art Nouveau*. "Beauty" or shirtwaist pins on original card (not shown). Sterling fronts.

Row 4:   BUCKLE, 2/pc., *Art Nouveau*. (Shown in closed position on PLATE 1). Open mechanism here shown, displays this unusual buckle styling. Oxidized silver w/open work ending w/peacock-eye accents. (Arts & Crafts)

HATPIN, *Art Nouveau*. Peacock-eye glass, bezel-set in sterling cage. Hallmarked: C.H. (Charles Horner), Chester, England.
(Mildred Combs Collection)

PLATE 24.

Row 1
Left to Right: WATCH CHAIN, *Art Nouveau*, gilt over brass, (*vermeil*).

PENDANT W/CHAIN, *Art Nouveau*, gold, (unmarked). French.

BROOCH, *Art Nouveau*, marked: S&P9575, hallmarked w/anchor (Birmingham).

Row 2
Left to Right: BROOCH, *Art Nouveau*, "Diana", gold set w/turquoise.

BROOCH, *Art Nouveau*, gold inscribed: "Lillian, L.A. 1906".

BROOCH, *Art Nouveau*, 14K, marked: L&A.

Row 3
Left to Right: BROOCH, *Art Nouveau*, gold w/three mine-cut diamonds.

PENDANT, *Art Nouveau*, Tiffany-type art glass scarab, bezel set in gold frame.

WATCH FOB, *Art Nouveau*, grosgrain ribbon w/locket, gilt over brass, marked inside locket: S & BL Co. w/star. (S. & B Lederer Co., Providence, R.I., trade-mark)

Row 4, Center: BROOCH, *Art Nouveau*, round medallion, inscribed, "Flore". Gold w/4 mine-cut diamonds set at woman's throat. Signed "F. Rasummy."

Row 5, Center: BELT BUCKLE, *Art Nouveau*; large, heavy gilt over brass. Signed: "A. Scher."

Row 5, Right: BROOCH, *Art Nouveau*, (shown atop grosgrain ribbon of watch fob). Gold set w/sapphire and pearls. (Papillion [Sherman Oaks]; Mike Iorg & Martin Wolpert Collection)

PLATE 25.

Row 1, Center: PENDANT, *Art Nouveau*, lady on Lily pad. 14K, enamel w/diamond.

Row 2, Left: PENDANT W/CHAIN, *Art Nouveau*, 14K gold w/diamond, and *baroque* pearl. (Not original chain.) Glasgow School.

Center: PENDANT W/CHAIN, *Art Nouveau*, 14K gold w/diamond, opals, and baroque pearl.

Right: PENDANT W/CHAIN, *Art Nouveau*, 14K set w/emeralds. Possibly portraying "The Butterfly Lady", dancer Löie Fuller.

Row 3, Left: PENDANT, *Art Nouveau*, 14K, w/diamond and emerald. (Extended Lily represents purity, innocence, Holy Virgin, The Annunciation.)

Center: PENDANT, *Art Nouveau*, 14K, w/diamonds and rubies.

Right: HOLDER, (Pendant-type for watch, fan, *lorgnette*). *Art Nouveau*, 14K w/diamond and emerald. (rare)

Row 4, Left: PENDANT, *Art Nouveau*, 14K, w/diamonds.

Center: PENDANT W/CHAIN, *Art Nouveau*, 14K, w/diamonds. Possibly fashioned after the fairy "Tinker Bell", from J.M. Barrie's "Peter Pan", (1904). Author Barrie was a contemporary of *Art Nouveau* artists. (Popular design being reproduced today.)

Right: PENDANT, *Art Nouveau*, 14K, mermaid, *plique-a-jour* enamel w/diamond.

Row 5, Left: PENDANT W/CHAIN, *Art Nouveau*, 14K, floral, *plique-a-jour* enamel w/diamond and blister pearl.

Center: PENDANT W/CHAIN, *Art Nouveau*, 14K, mythological beast w/diamonds and rubies. Possibly dragon w/sword depicting medieval story of St. George and the slain dragon. (Aesthetic Period)

Right: PENDANT W/CHAIN, *Art Nouveau*, 14K, *plique-a-jour* enamel w/diamond and blister pearl.
(Jenny Biddle Collection/Cape Cottage Antiques)

PLATE 26.

Left to Right: BROOCH, *Art Nouveau*, 14K, 1¼" overall, w/3 emeralds and one diamond.

BROOCH, *Art Nouveau*, 14K, 1-1/8" painted enamel accents on animal and floral motifs, typical of Arts and Crafts Movement. Cabachon-cut and highly polished ½" malachite gemstone. Celtic influence.

PENDANT, *Art Nouveau*, 14K, 1½" overall snake motif w/2 ruby eyes, 1 diamond and 4 emeralds. Although the serpent in some cultures is considered an evil omen, because of its shedding skin, it also represents the "casting off" or change in spirit.
(Jenny Biddle Collection/Cape Cottage Antiques)

PLATE 27.

BROOCH OR SCARF PIN, *Art Nouveau*. 14K, 4" long Asp, w/chased and embossed head, accented by ruby eye and 3/8" bezel-set faceted amethyst held between serpent's fangs. The snake, in many myths and religious cults, is symbolic of rejuvination and immortality, because it sheds or "renews" its skin.
(Jenny Biddle Collection/Cape Cottage Antiques)

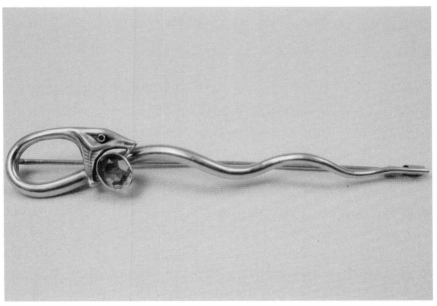

PLATE 28.

Row 1:   NECKLACE, Art Deco. Chased gilt over brass, Egyptian influence in geometric line w/wired blue glass beads and hand-blown free-form iridescent glass drops. Circa 1920, Bohemian *Secession*.
(Author's Collection)

Row 2, Left: WOMAN'S WATCH, *Art Nouveau*, 18K, w/black enameled rim and case. Face inscribed: "Tiffany and Company". 22" black silk ribbon hangs on gold loop, (not shown).

Center: BRACELET W/SLIDES, *Art Nouveau*. 14K gold assorted slides set with diamonds and sapphires.

Right: WATCH, Art Deco. 14K pink gold set w/diamonds and rubies. Note unusual bracelet-clasp.

Row 3, Left: KNIFE W/PENCIL, Art Deco. 14K w/chased and engraved frame. (Late Deco)

Center: MONEY CLIP, Art Deco. 14K, w/U.S. dollar goldpiece dated 1853. Inscribed: "To Dreamer from Bing". Gift from Bing Crosby to his make-up man.

Right: TIE CLIP, Art Deco. 14K, w/sapphires. (Late Deco)

Row 4:   WATCH CHAIN W/SLIDE. *Art Nouveau*, 23" lady's chain w/swivel clasp, rolled & plated gold, w/¾" slide set w/turquoise.
(Author's Collection)
(Jenny Biddle Collection/Cape Cottage Antiques, unless otherwise noted)

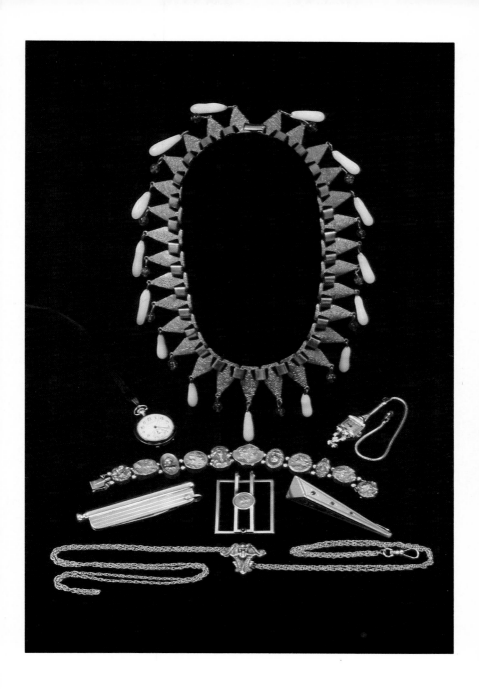

PLATE 29.

Row 1:   BROOCH, *Art Nouveau*, ¾" gilt over brass w/engraved Peacock feathers, Cranes, and Lilies. Designs in high relief, bezel-set w/peacock-eye glass accents.

Row 2, Left: BUCKLE, *Art Nouveau*, oxidized German silver w/lacquered brass.

Right: HATPIN, *Art Nouveau*, gilt over brass. Egyptian motif accented w/peacock-eye glass. Steel pin-shank.

Row 3, Left: BROOCH, *Art Nouveau*, gilt over brass, stylized falcon w/bezel set peacock-eye glass accent.

Right: BUCKLE, *Art Nouveau*, die-stamped and wire-worked frame, engraved and accented w/simulated jade.

Row 4:   HATPIN, *Art Nouveau*, Cabachon cut simulated jade, bezel-set atop gilt over brass pierced and engraved mounting. Gilded pin shank. Egyptian motif.
(Mildred Combs Collection)

PLATE 30.

Top to Bottom: BAR PIN, Art Deco, platinum w/*pavé* set diamonds and center diamond & sapphire.

BROOCH, *Art Nouveau*, Egyptian influence, gilt over brass w/glass imitation stones in headdress.

NECKLACE, *Art Nouveau*, marked: *Symmetalic* - Sterling - 14K, set w/moonstones & amethysts. (*Jugendstil* or *Secession*, Glasgow influence)

BROOCH, *Art Nouveau,* marked: Sterling, w/cabachon cut amethysts and pearl drop.

PENDANT, *Art Nouveau*, depicting Shakespeare's tragic Ophelia, ("Hamlet"). Bedecked with flowers, the hapless Opehlia drowns in the stream amidst Water-Lilies, symbol of her purity. Copper w/silver and gold wash; blue enameling simulates rippling waters. (Aesthetic influence) (Papillion [Sherman Oaks]; Mike Iorg & Martin Wolpert Collection)

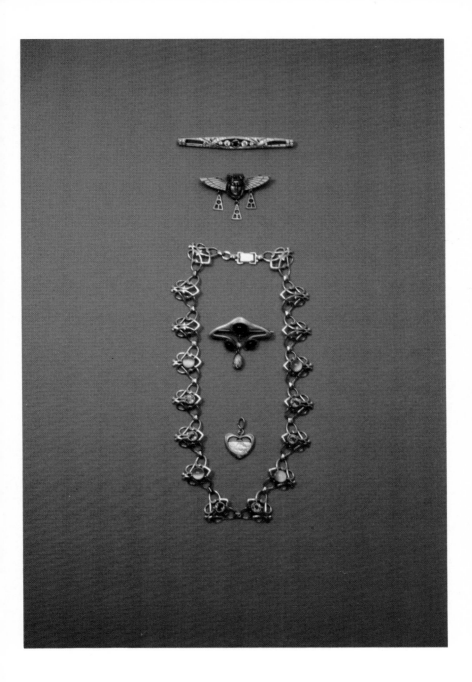

PLATE 31.

Top: ORNAMENTAL COMB, *Art Nouveau*, 7¼" wide x 6", piercework plastic w/imitation blue stones.

Center: BROOCH, *Art Nouveau*, gilt over brass w/faceted *faux* amethyst.

Bottom;   SIDE COMB, *Art Nouveau*, genuine tortoise w/applied metallic decoration and simulated gemstones.

Left: NECKLACE, Art Deco, Bohemian design, molded glass.

Right: NECKLACE, Art Deco, Bohemian cut and faceted glass. (Mildred Combs Collection)

PLATE 32.

Left: PENDANT W/CHAIN, *Art Nouveau*, 14K, 1¼" Owl in flight w/2 emeralds and 1 diamond. It was believed that Owls w/outstretched wings protected one from lightning. The Owl was also associated w/night and wisdom, the latter from "Athena's Bird" — the Owl. (Athena is the Goddess of Wisdom)

Center: BROOCH W/HINGED pendant loop, *Art Nouveau*, 14K, 7/8" overall miniature in exquisite detail of Mercury's winged helmet and running feet, symbolizing speedy and continuous messages of good fortune.

Right: PENDANT W/CHAIN, *Art Nouveau*, 14K, unusual pair of profiles joined together w/opal. Possibly "The Twin Goddesses", one representing vegetation of the fields, the other the fruits of the arbor — both symbolizing eternal evolution of all animal and human life.
(Jenny Biddle Collection/Cape Cottage Antiques)

PLATE 33.

Top:
CHATELAINE Hook w/PURSE, Art Nouveau. Sterling frame and silver mesh w/sterling embossed chatelaine belt hook attached to chain. Note how design on waist-band hook and purse frame are matched maidens.

Row 2, Left:
BROOCH, Art Nouveau. Sterling w/gold wash set w/diamonds and Persian turquoise accent in hair.

Right:
LOCKET, Art Nouveau, heavy sterling w/turquoise accents. Intricate repousse work. Unger Bros., Newark, N.J.

Center:
BROOCH (on mesh purse), Art Nouveau. Large, exceptional depth achieved by embossing and repousse work in sterling. Unger Bros., Newark, N.J.

Bottom:
NECKLACE, Art Nouveau, typical German "Jugenstil" design; Theodore Fahrner, enamel on sterling, w/sterling chains.
(Papillon [Sherman Oaks]; Mike Iorg & Martin Wolpert Collection)

PLATE 34.

Row 1, Left: PENDANT, Art Deco, *vermeil* (silver over copper), enamel.

Center: PENDANT W/CHAIN, Art Deco, sterling w/marcasites and enamel. Transitional piece.

Right: PENDANT, Art Deco, enamel on sterling.

Row 2:   BRACELET, Art Deco, enamel on sterling.

Row 3:   NECKLACE, Art Deco, enameled *vermeil*, (silver on copper).

Row 4:   Two BROOCHES, Art Deco. Highly stylized golfers, enamel on sterling.

Row 5:   NECKLACE, Art Deco, silver on copper w/enameling the epitome of Deco design and technique.
(Papillion [Sherman Oaks]; Mike Iorg & Martin Wolpert Collection)

73

PLATE 35.

Left:
PENDANT W/CHAIN, *Art Nouveau*. 14K, nude among Water-Lilies. In ancient mythology, the Water-Lily (sacred Lotus), is associated with female fertility and resurrection of Life. Each embossed Lily is set w/diamonds and emeralds.

Center:
LAVALIER, Art Nouveau, 14K, product typical of the Aesthetic and Arts and Crafts simplicity. 1¼" wide w/3/8" jade drop w/2 *baroque* pearls. Applied enamel.

Right:
PENDANT W/CHAIN, *Art Nouveau*, 14K, bust of woman in floral design frame, adorned w/diamond.
(Jenny Biddle Collection/Cape Cottage Antiques)

PLATE 36.

Top: COIN PURSE, *Art Nouveau*, sterling, hinged top disc w/pouch of cut and crochet steel beads. Fine *repousse* floral design.

Center: PURSE, *Art Nouveau*, sterling frame w/inscription of owner's name. German silver mesh.

                BUCKLE (on mesh background), *Art Nouveau*, swirling Irises in marked sterling. Buckle is exceptionally large. (Mildred Combs Collection)

PLATE 37.

Top: BROOCH, *Art Nouveau*, German silver. Unique design, "Blowing Bubbles".

Row 2, Left: BROOCH, *Art Nouveau*, French silver mark. "Diana" w/*repousse* and open work.

Center: BROOCH, *Art Nouveau*, marked: Sterling silver trademark. Large overall w/*repousse* and open work.

Right: WATCH FOB, *Art Nouveau*. French silver mark w/artist's signature: "Dropsey". (This piece now being reproduced.)

Row 3, Left: BROOCH, *Art Nouveau*, marked: Sterling. Chased and embossed. Large dimension.

Right: BROOCH, *Art Nouveau*. Very large and weighty silver in high relief w/intricate open work. Marked: Sterling 12/3 Kerr (William W. Kerr & Co., Newark, N.J.) (Now being reproduced.)

Row 4, Left: BROOCH, *Art Nouveau*. Symbolic half-moon and Bat. Sterling w/gold wash. Maker's mark: Frank M. Whiting & Co., Attleboro, Mass.

Center: BROOCH, *Art Nouveau*. Sterling w/maker's mark: La Pierre Mfg. Co., Newark, N.J.

Right: BROOCH, *Art Nouveau*. Sterling w/unidentifiable maker's mark.
(Papillion [Sherman Oaks]; Mike Iorg & Martin Wolpert Collection)

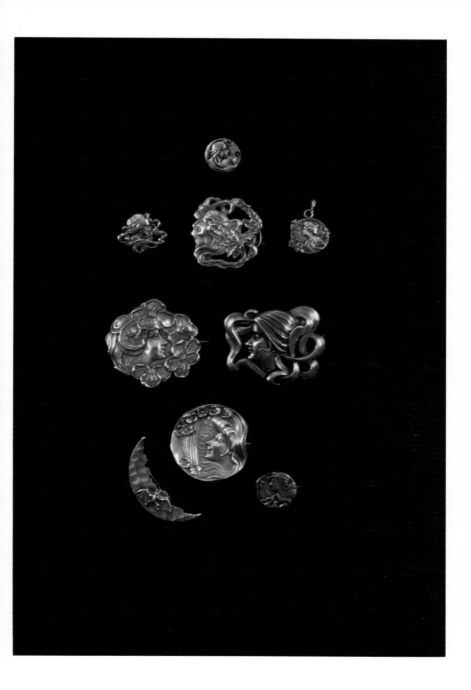

PLATE 38.

STICKPIN, sterling, *Art Nouveau*, 14K, 1" overall, woman in winged helmet depicting the Greek god Hermes, messenger of good fortune and eloquence. The headband is set with 3 diamonds and 2 rubies. Two inch pin-shank.
(Jenny Biddle Collection/Cape Cottage Antiques)

PLATE 39.

BROOCH, *Art Nouveau*. Gold w/*plique-a-jour* enameling w/granular work. Rubies and diamonds set in gypsy mountings. Carved ivory face. Designed by Eugene Feuillatre, who worked with Rene Lalique. (See contrast of *Art Nouveau* design with Art Deco necklace on PLATE 49).
(Jenny Biddle Collection/Cape Cottage Antiques)

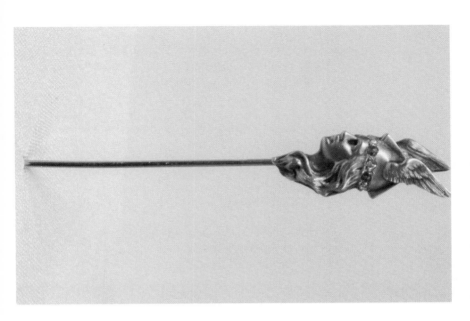

PLATE 40.

Unique button collection, (circa 1870-1930), representing Aesthetic, Arts & Crafts, "high" *Art Nouveau*, and Art Deco designs and motifs. Sizes: ¼" - 2".

Row 1
Left to Right: Metallic Iris w/mother-of-pearl; enameled brass; sterling w/opal; art glass w/goldstone; pierced *champleve* enamel.

Row 2, Left: "Ivy" portrait, *Limoges* enamel.
Center: Painted enamel violets.
Right: "Yris" portrait, *Limoges* enamel.

Row 3, Left: *Basse-taille* and *champleve* enamelled carnation.
Center: Large Bat in pressed horn.
Right: *Champleve* enamel, Poppies.

Row 4, Left: Iris in matte *champleve* enamels.
Center: Painted enamel square-shape (shown at angle).
Right: *Champleve* enamelled floral.

Row 5, Left: Enamelled Water-Lilies.
Right: Pierced enamel.

Row 6, Left: *Champleve* enamels in typical Deco colors.
Center: Glass w/silver deposit.
Right: *Champleve* enamel.

Row 7, Left: Glass w/silver deposit.
Center: *Champleve* enamel.
Right: Celluloid.

Row 8, Left: *Champleve* enamel, oriental influence.
Center: Pierced copper
Right: *Champleve* enamel.
            (Mildred Combs Collection)

83

PLATE 41.

CAMEO PENDANT W/CHAIN, *Art Nouveau*, 14K
Roman gold-framed helmet shell, carved cameo, w/14K
gold chain. Rare design and shape.
(Mildred Combs Collection)

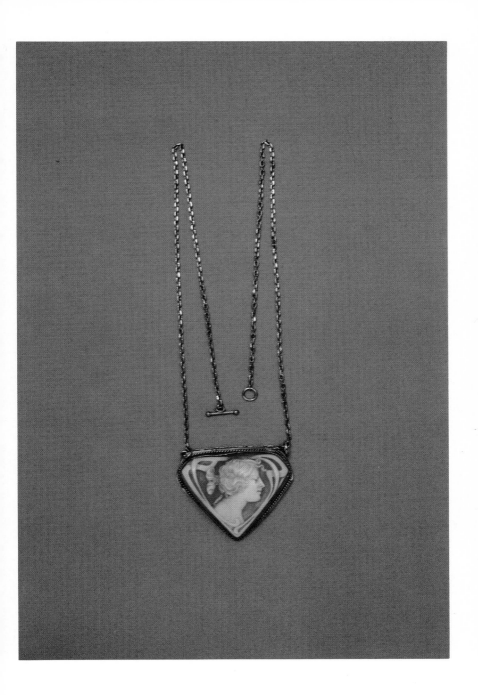

PLATE 42.

Row 1:   HATPIN, Art Deco, circa 1920. Egyptian influence. Brass w/glass simulated malachite.

Row 2:   BUCKLE, 2/pc., Art Deco, Arabic influence in design. Chased brass on plastic.

Row 3:   BRACELET, Art Deco. Chinese influence. Copper and oxidized silver w/molded glass simulated carnelian.

Row 4:   BROOCH, *Art Nouveau*. Japanese influence. Gilt over brass w/simulated topaz.
(Mildred Combs Collection)

PLATE 43.

Row 1
Left to Right: PENDANT W/CHAIN, *Art Nouveau*. Favored "floating blue" *basse-taille* enamel on sterling. Hallmarked: Charles Horner (England)

BROOCH, *Art Nouveau*, Charles Horner, enamel on sterling.

PENDANT W/CHAIN, *Art Nouveau*, Charles Horner, enamel on sterling.

Row 2
Left to Right: BROOCH, *Art Nouveau*, Charles Horner, *champleve* enamel on sterling.

PENDANT, *Art Nouveau*, peacock-blue *basse-taille* enamel, sterling w/gold wash, w/*baroque* pearl drop. Charles Horner.

BROOCH, *Art Nouveau*, winged scarab, enamel on sterling. Charles Horner.

Row 3
Left to Right: PENDANT, *Art Nouveau*, *basse-taille* enamel, English hallmark, sterling w/initials: J & E.

PENDANT, *Art Nouveau*, luminous enamel on sterling w/lustrous mother-of-pearl insert.

PENDANT, *Art Nouveau*, Murrle, Bennett Co., (English). Sterling w/gold wash and baroque pearl drop.
(Papillion [Sherman Oaks], Mike Iorg & Martin Wolpert Collection)

PLATE 44.

Row 1, Left: HATPIN, *Art Nouveau*, individually rivited black faceted glass on wire frame. Jablonec, Czech., Early *Secession*.
(Author's Collection)

Center: HATPIN, Art Deco, enameled mercury glass on sliding pin-shank.
(Author's Collection)

Right: *LAVALIERE*, *Art Nouveau*, Jablonec rivited cut black glass on wire frame.
(Author's Collection)

Row 2, Left: RING, Art Deco, 18K w/sapphires & diamonds.

Center: RING, Art Deco, 14K w/sapphires and diamonds.

Right: RING, Art Deco, 14K w/sapphires & diamonds.

Row 3, Left to Right: RINGS, Art Deco: sterling w/marcasites & amethysts; sterling w/marcasites & onyx; sterling w/chrysoprase.

Row 4, Left: RING, Art Deco, 14K w/sapphires & diamonds.

Center: RING, Art Deco, platinum w/diamond & onyx.

Right: RING, Art Deco, 18K w/sapphires & diamonds.

Row 5:   BRACELET, Art Deco, 14K w/diamonds & emerald.

Row 6:   PENDANT W/CHAIN, Art Deco, platinum w/diamonds.

Row 7:   BRACELET, Art Deco, sterling w/green and black enameling.
(Jenny Biddle Collection/Cape Cottage Antiques, unless otherwise noted.)

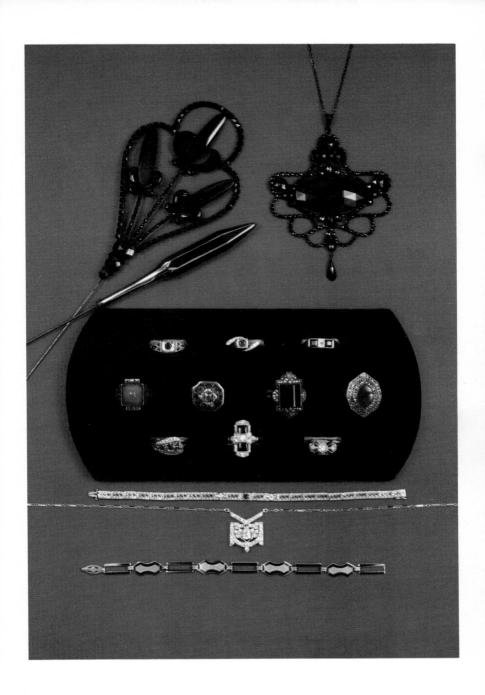

91

PLATE 45.

Row 1: PENDANT W/CHAIN, *Art Nouveau*, pr. of dragonflies in profile, carved horn accented by claw-set moonstone. French, possibly Lucien Gaillard.

Row 2, Left: BROOCH, *Art Nouveau*, bumble bee in flight. Carved horn.

Right: BROOCH, *Art Nouveau*, dragonfly in flight. Carved horn.

Row 3: BROOCH, *Art Nouveau*, carved horn butterfly w/mock Persian turquoise accent.

Row 4: BROOCH, *Art Nouveau*, dragonfly in carved horn.

Row 5, Left: ORNAMENTAL HAIR COMB, *Art Nouveau, faux* tortoise set w/blue foil-backed brilliants.

Right: DECORATIVE HAIR PIN, *Art Nouveau*, heavy tortoise shell, carved poppy blossom.
(Papillion [Sherman Oaks]; Mike Iorg & Martin Wolpert Collection)

PLATE 46.

Top: BUTTON, *Art Nouveau*, English hallmarked: sterling, (Birmingham, 1907), w/initials: W.H.H.

Center, Top: HATPIN, *Art Nouveau*, sterling, hallmarked: Birmingham, 1909. Peacock-blue enamel. Signed: J.E.

Center, Bottom: PIN, *Art Nouveau*, lace or "beauty" pin for shirtwaist collar or blouse. Sterling hallmark: Chester, Charles Horner.

Bottom: NECKLACE, *Art Nouveau*. Peacock-blue "floating blue" enamel on silver w/fresh-water blister pearls. Attributed to Liberty and Co., England. Typical Celtic design influence. (Mildred Combs Collection)

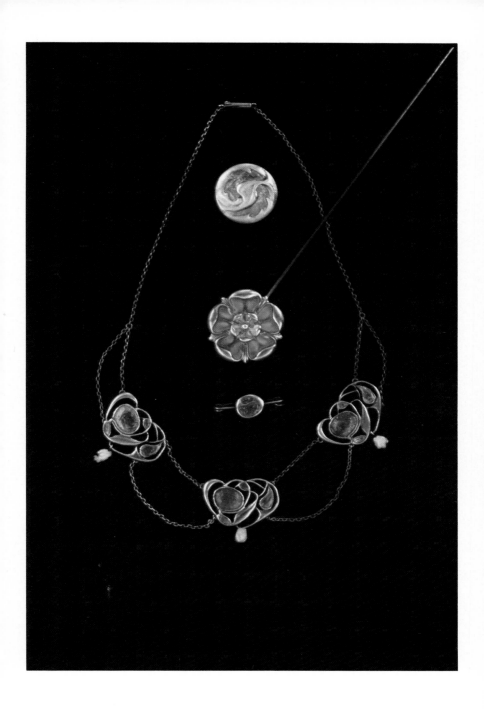

95

PLATE 47.

Row 1, Left: BROOCH, Art Deco, polished onyx w/marcasites set into sterling w/jadite center stone. (French)

Right: PENDANT w/chain, Art Deco, sterling frame set w/faceted topaz color glass and marcasites. (Bohemian)

Row 2: SCARF PIN, *Art Nouveau*, symbolic Bat in oxidized German silver, highly engraved w/hollow back and *repousse* work. Revival of interest in the bizarre, and in the "Bat Man" TV character, heightens demand and market value of this "cultist" motif. Five Bats symbolize the five blessings: age, health, wealth, virtue, and a natural death. (Chinese)

Row 3: *LAVALIERE, Art Nouveau*, gilt over brass, oxidized, set w/green matrix turquoise. Clasp marked: F. & B. (Theodore W. Foster & Bro. Co., Providence, R.I., trademark)

Row 4: STICKPINS (6), *Art Nouveau*, all gold carat, w/ornamental heads and gold pin-shanks. French *Art Nouveau* motifs.Very collectible.
(Papillion [Sherman Oaks]; Mike Iorg & Martin Wolpert Collection)

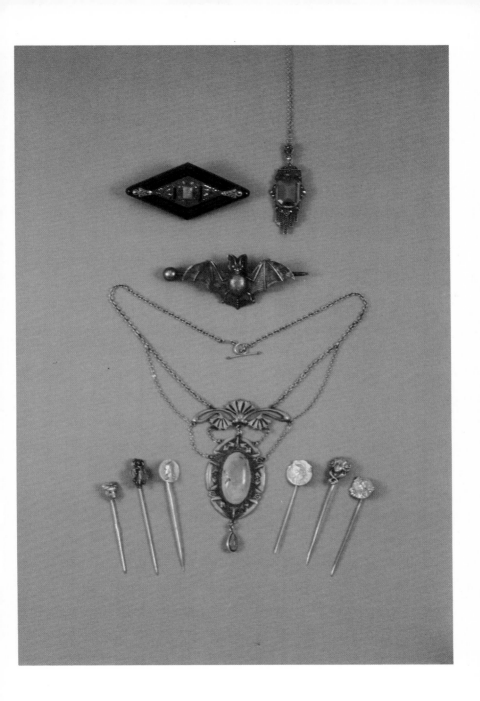

PLATE 48.

Row 1:   BUCKLE, one piece, *Art Nouveau*, hand rivited cut steel in patterned Bird of Paradise design. Buckle for belt or sash.

Row 2:   Pr. SHOE BUCKLES, *Art Nouveau*, hand cut steel, individually rivited to frame. Transitional Deco pattern. "Made in France"

Row 3, Left: BELT BUCKLE, 2/pc., *Art Nouveau*, die-stamped, cut and polished open work, w/cut steel on brass, grograin insert.

Center: BROOCH, *Art Nouveau*, Tortoise shell w/*pique* work, etched floral motif in oxidized silver, set w/borders of marcasites. Marked: *Depose*. (French)
(Author's Collection)

Right: BELT BUCKLE, 2/pc., *Art Nouveau*, cut and individually rivited cut steel, *pavé* set.

Row 4:   Pr. SHOE BUCKLES, *Art Nouveau*, cut steel individually rivited and set on frame w/grograin backing.

Row 5:   Pr. SHOE CLIPS, Art Deco, cut steel on white alloy. Marked: Made in France.

Row 6:   BUTTON, *Art Nouveau*, brass w/cut steel sets and painted enamel.
(Mildred Combs Collection, except where otherwise noted.)

PLATE 49.

Row 1
Left to Right: PENDANT, *Art Nouveau*. Gold, faced w/platinum and set w/diamonds & pearls.(*Nouveau* to Deco transitional piece.)

PENDANT W/CHAIN, *Art Nouveau*. 14K gold w/rubies and diamonds.

PENDANT W/CHAIN, *Art Nouveau*. 14K gold w/opal.

PENDANT W/CHAIN, *Art Nouveau*, 14K gold w/diamonds.

PENDANT w/CHAIN, *Art Nouveau*, 14K gold w/seed pearls and pearl drop. (Arts & Crafts influence)

Row 2:   BUCKLE, *Art Nouveau*, Pansy motif in *matte* enamel. (Mildred Combs Collection)

Row 3
Left to Right: PENDANT, *Art Nouveau*, 14K gold w/blister pearls.

LAVALIERE, Art Nouveau, 14K gold, set w/peridots, pearls and ruby.

PENDANT W/CHAIN, *Art Nouveau*. 14K gold, set w/amethyst and pearls.

Row 4:   2/pc. BUCKLE, *Art Nouveau*, oxidized metal, Japanese *cloisonne*, counter-enameled on reverse side. (Mildred Combs Collection)

Row 5:   BROOCH, Art Deco. Tortoise shell w/*pique* work, mounted on plastic, set w/brilliants.
(Author's Collection)
(Jenny Biddle Collection/Cape Cottage Antiques, unless otherwise noted.)

PLATE 50.

Row 1:   DECORATIVE SEW-ON BUCKLE, Art Deco. Peacock motif, painted plastic, set w/colored brilliants.

Row 2:   NECKLACE, *Art Nouveau*, transitional piece. Green Czech, glass w/enameled leaves. (*Secessionist* influence)

Row 3
Left to Right: BUCKLE, one/piece, *Art Nouveau*. Japanese *cloisonne*, Iris motif, counter-enameled on reverse side.

BUCKLE, 2/pc., *Art Nouveau*. Japanese *cloisonne* w/counter enameling on reverse side.

HATPIN (head only), *Art Nouveau*. *Champleve* enameled figural butterfly.

Row 4
Left to Right: BROOCH, *Art Nouveau*. Marked: Sterling, GI(925), Georg Jensen.

BROOCH, *Art Nouveau*. Obverse side inscribed: "Diane". Reverse side marked: Sterling w/Unger Bros., Newark, N.J. trade-mark.

BROOCH, Art Deco. Marked: Sterling, NJ Georg Jensen. (Mildred Combs Collection)

SECTION III

CHAPTER I
SOURCES OF ECLECTIC DESIGNS AND MOTIFS FOR THE "NEW ART" JEWELRY

CHAPTER II
ART NOUVEAU AND ART DECO JEWELRY MATERIALS

CHAPTER III
CONTRASTS

CHAPTER IV
*NATURALISTIC MOTIFS OF *ART NOUVEAU* AND ART DECO (including Arts & Crafts Movement & Aesthetic Period)

CHAPTER I
SOURCES OF ECLECTIC DESIGNS AND
MOTIFS FOR THE "NEW ART" JEWELRY

African *
Symbolism
Masks
Symbolic Gods
Jungle Beasts
Exotic Birds

American Indian *
Baskets
Beadwork
Blankets
Maze Designs
Pueblo Pottery
Sand Painting
Totem Poles

Mayan & Pre-Columbian *
Artifacts
Aztec Temples
Eagles
Geometric Florals
Geometric Patterns
    of Gods/Man/Monster
Symbolism
Sun Disc

Far East: Arabic, Indian, Persian, Turkish, etc.
Assyrian Wings
Islamic Designs
The Koran
Paisley Patterns
Temples
Arabesques
Medallions
Mythical Creatures
Rosettes
Zodiac

Egyptian
Eye of Horis
Pharohs & Tombs
Hawk
Pyramids
Papyrus
Sacred Asp
Scarab (Beetle)
Sphinxes
Salamander
Hieroglyphics
Tutankhamen (1922)*

Japanese
Bamboo
Beetles
Buddhist Symbols
Cranes
Dragonfly
Fan
Feathers
Fir Cones
Lotus
Iris
Wisteria
Pagoda
Sun Disc
Snails
Tsuba (Sword Guard)
Crests
Tortoise
Two-dimensional
    graphics
Artist, Hokusai

Chinese

Abstracts
Bat
Butterflies
Chinese Ideographs
Chrysanthemums
Coins
Dragon
Fish
Lattice Designs
Lion
Lotus Flower
Narcissus (Chinese
  sacred Lily)
Peacocks
Phoenixes
Serpents
Temples
Tigers
Tortoise

European & Russian

Ancient Egyptian Art
Architecture/Horta
Arts & Crafts Movement,
  (Wm. Morris & Co.)
Bauhaus (Weimer, Germany)*
Bluebird
Botany
Butterflies
Celtic Design, (Glasgow School)
Cubism*
Dadaism, Surrealism*

Eagle
Falcon (Hawk)
Fantasy & Mythology:
  Fairies, Mermaids, Nymphs,
  Satyrs, Dragon, Gryphon, Vampires
Female Nudes/Torso
Flappers, Harlequins*
Impressionism*
Lower Organic Life
Marine Life: Snails,
  Sea Shells, etc.
Medieval Interlacements
Medieval "Romanticism" &
  "Innocence"
Medusas
Metamorphisis
Moorish (Spain)*
Mystic Symbols
"Orientalia"
Posters/Graphics: Beardsley,
  Mucha, Toulouse-Lautrec,
  Bonnard, Grasset, etc.
  (See Thumbnail Sketches)
Russian Ballet*
Speed Symbols*
Symbolism
Tendrils of Hair
Uninhibited sensuality, "high"
  Art Nouveau, (France)
Water

*Primarily Art Deco

CHAPTER II
ART NOUVEAU AND ART DECO
JEWELRY MATERIALS

Metals & Ores
Aluminum*
Copper
Gold
Pewter
Platinum*
Silver
Steel*

Metallic
Alloys
Brass
Chrome*
White Gold*

Gems &
Gemstones
Agate
Amethyst
Black Onyx*
Cat's Eye
Chrysoberyl
Chrysoprase
Citrine
Diamond
Emerald
Jade
Jadite
Jasper
Jet
Lapis Lazuli

Malachite
Marcasite
Moonstone
Obsidian*
Olivine*
 (Chrysolite)
Onyx*
Opal
Peridot
 (Chrysolite)
Rock Crystal
 (Quartz)
Rose Quartz
Ruby
Sapphire
Sodalite
Topaz
Turquoise
 (Persian)
Turquoise Matrix*
Zircon

Natural
Elements
Abalone Shell
 (Mexican)
Amber
Bone*
Coral
Ebony*

Hardrock
Horse Hide*
Ivory
 (tusk/tooth)
Marble
Mother-of-Pearl
Sea Shells
 (Helmet &
 Conch)
Tortoise-shell
Wood*

Man-Made
Materials
Bakelite*
Brilliants*
Celluloid*
Enamels
Frosted Rock
 Crystal*
Glass: iridescent,
 molded,
 faceted,
 "camphor", etc.
Paste (imitation
 gems &
 gemstones &
 pate-de-verre
Painted Glass*
Plastics*
Synthetic Gems*

* Primarily Art Deco and late *Nouveau*.
Note: Frosted rock crystal/diamonds and platinum/plastics, were given
 equal status during Art Deco design period.

CHAPTER III
CONTRASTS

Aesthetic Movement (Great Britain)
Morality & Medieval "Romanticism"
Crusades, religious revival
Hand-crafted work*
Curved geometric lines w/Medieval themes
Gentle beasts
Unexaggerated florals
Curved natural forms
Sentimental Themes: Knights & Ladies *"Faire"*
Elegant literal designs for both settings and stones
Gems cut *en cabachon*
Virginal maidens w/single blossom in hand or hair
Purity & child-like innocence
Simplicity w/richness in design
Figurative work: pre-Raphaelite influence
    *"Avoid machine-made jewelry, it lacks originality."
    (*The Studio Magazine*, Vol. 37, 1906)

Jugenstil (Germany) and **Secession** (Austria & Czech.)**
Cube
Rectangle
Untraditional concepts in art's form and function
Spiral
Squares
Circles with perforations
Circles within circles or squares
Dots
Scrolling with wire
Checkerboard
        **Primarily influenced by the Glasgow School
Scandinavia
Influenced by the British Arts & Crafts Movement and the "Glasgow Four"

French & Belgium *Art Nouveau*
Female nudes
Eroticism
Undulating curves
Voluptuous sculpturing

Female torso combined w/beauty
   of nature
Curvilinear lines
Arabesques
Embryology
Billowing/wispy "smoke" lines
Pulsations
Metamorphosis of organic life
Ornamental "nervous" line
Symbolism
Artistic self-indulgence
Mysticism
Unrolling spirals and free form
Fantasy
Mystery
The exaggerated line
Enigma
Japanese two-dimensional graphics
Symbolic pictographs
Eclectic influence prevails
Sensual, uninhibited, "decadent"

American *Art Nouveau*
Influenced by British Arts &
   Crafts Movement and French
   "high" *Art Nouveau.*

British Arts & Crafts Movement
Beaten metal work
Hand-made vs. Machine-made**
Restrained abstract design
Celtic Cross, late 18th C.**
Celtic lines, circles, rosettes,
   sculptured curves, asymmetric,
   auricular (ear lobe) style**
Convulsive outlines
Expressionism vs. Impressionism
Whiplash lines
Austerity of design**
Curlicues
Restrained interpretations
   of nature
Arabesques
Stylization of figures**

Ovals & curved bands**
Flat curves**
Designs for machine-made mass
 production
Eggshape
Discs
Absence of female nudes
    ** Primarily Glasgow School

Art Deco (pioneered by Vienna *Secession*, Glasgow School, and further
 implemented by *Bauhaus* schools in Weimer and Dessau; the latter laud-
 ed the virtues of revitalizing new liberties in artistic license and design
 concepts)
Rectilinear forms
Enamel designs in stark red, black and deep lush blue
Symbols of streamlining, speed, electricity, transportation
Checkerboard (black and white)
Non-figurative design
Pavé set stones
Functional "confident" line
Painted glass w/metal
Non-passant beasts
Cubism, Impressionism, Exoticism, Eclecticism
Geometric designs in various proportions: triangles, squares, diagonals,
 rectangles, octagons, hexagons and circles
Flappers
"Orientalia"
"Beauty and the Beast"

CHAPTER IV
*NATURALISTIC MOTIFS OF *ART NOUVEAU* AND ART DECO (including Arts & Crafts Movement & Aesthetic Period)

Botanical

Arrowroot
Bamboo
Berries
Bryony
Cattelya
Chrysanthemum
Daffodil
Fern
Fir Cone
Fuchia
Hibiscus
Iris
Jonquil
Leaves* *
Lily-of-the-valley
Lotus (Water Lilies)
Mushrooms
Narcissus
Oak
Orchid
Pansy
Papyrus
Poppy
Seaweed
Seeds
Sun Flower
Sweet Pea
Thistle
Tulip
Vines
Weeds
Wisteria

Birds & Beast

Antelope* *
Bat* *
Bluebird
Crane
Eagle
Falcon* *
Hawk* *
Peacock
Swan
Faun
Lion* *

Reptiles

Lizards
Salamanders* *
Snakes* *
Tortoise

Insects

Beetles* *
  (Scarab)
Butterflies
Dragonflies

Marine Life

Fish (Goldfish
  or Carp)
Frog
Oyster
Snail* *

Strictly Deco Motifs
Beasts* * *

Antelopes
Borzois (dog)

Elephant
Greyhound (dog)
Leopard
Panther
Tiger

Birds

Parrot
Vulture

Abstract

Bubbles
Fountains
Racing Clouds
Rising Sun
Speed Motifs
Sports
Streamlined Configurations
Wind-blown Hair,
  (streamlined)
Waterfalls

*These motifs appear in a more abstract style in all German-speaking countries.

* *Highly stylized and streamlined in Art Deco.

* * *In depicting wild animals, *Nouveau* portrayed "the gentle beast"; Deco, the non-passant, aggressive animal.

SECTION IV

CHAPTER I
THUMBNAIL SKETCHES
JEWELERS - JEWELRY DESIGNERS - MAKERS - MANUFACTURERS - RETAILERS

CHAPTER II
GLOSSARY OF JEWELRY TERMS AND TYPES, INCLUDING PRONUNCIATION

CHAPTER I
THUMBNAIL SKETCHES
JEWELERS - JEWELRY DESIGNERS - MAKERS - MANUFACTURERS - RETAILERS

Alvin Mfg. Co., (Sag Harbor, New York), sterling *art nouveau* pieces.

Ashbee, Charles Robert, (1863-1942), (British) Arts & Crafts jewelry designer and maker. Designed jewels executed by The Guild of Handicraft. Exhibited Vienna *Secession*, 1900 & 1906; British Decorative Arts, (Paris, 1914 exhibition). Major influence.

Attleboro Mfg. Co., (Attleboro, Mass.), sterling *art nouveau* jewelry.

Aucoc, Andre, jewelry firm (Paris); Louis Aucoc gave apprenticeship, 1876, to Rene Lalique.

Bablet, Paul, (b1889 - ?), jewelry designer and craftsman.

Bailey, Banks and Biddle Co., (Phila., Pa.), Jewelry firm.

Baltimore Sterling Silver Buckle Co., (Maryland), *art nouveau* jewelry.

Bastard, Georges, (b. ? - died 1939), Frenchman who specialized in modern and art deco motifs executed in ivory, mother-of-pearl, horn, wood, crystal; also precious stones and ores.

Bass, E & J (New York), silver plated jewelry.

Batchedler, Ernest A., American designer who studied in Birmingham, England, and was influenced by Arts & Crafts movement. Authored "The Principles of Design", (1904) and stimulated the American Arts & Crafts movement, particularly in Minnesota.

Behrens, Peter, (1868-1940), German designer who was a founding member of the 1893 Munich *Sezession*.

Bennett Merwin Silver Co., (New Milford, Conn.), sterling.

Berge, Henri, French glassmaker who made models for casting in *pate-de-verre* by A. Walter, (1908). (See Plate 12)

Bindesboll, Thorvald, *(1846-1908),* Danish jewelry designer.

Bing, Marcel, (C. 1840-1905), brother of Samuel Bing, founder of *"L'Art Nouveau"*, Paris. Marcel Bing made brooches and pendants using gilt copper, *cloisonne* enamels and "inferior" stones.

Bing, Samuel, who opened his *"Galleries de l'Art Nouveau"*, (Paris, 1895), following his 1893 visit to the Chicago World's Fair. His shop became the showplace for "modern" designers and jewelers.

Blackington, R & Co., (N. Attleboro, Mass.) sterling.

Bolin, W.A., Jewelry manufacturers, founded in 1845; made costly jewelry for the Russian Imperial Court.

Bonner, Houghton Maurice, British designer "commercial" jewelry.

Boucheron, Frederick, (1830-1902), founded French jewelry firm *"Maison Boucheron"*; produced both *nouveau* and deco designs by Cauvin and L. Hirtz, as well a works of other jewelry designers.

Boutet de Monvel, Charles, French jeweler.

Brandt, Edgar, metalworker who also made Art Deco jewelry.

Brandt, Paul-Emile (C. 1900) Swiss jewelry designer.

Brangwyn, Sir Frank, from 1882-1884 worked with Morris & Co. designing tapestries; 1885 exhibited at Royal Academy and was appointed R.A. (1919). Designed metalwork and jewelry, influenced by African, Oriental and Spanish art. Assisted in decorating Samuel Bing's *"Maison de l'Art Nouveau"*, (1895); stained glass for New York's Tiffany & Co., ("Picking Gourds" 1899); collaborated w/Jose Maria Sert and Diego Rivera in decorating New York's Rockefeller Center.

Brateau, Jules-Paul, (1844-1923), French jeweler who worked in *pate-de-verre* media, C1910.

Bristol Mfg. Co., (Attleboro, Mass.), German Silver/mesh bags.

Burges, William, (1827-1881), British jewelry designer and jeweler whose "mixed media" ornaments may have inspired some of Henry Wilson's work which was to come years later.

Burne-Jones, Edward, British jewelry designer.

Canadian Jewelers, Ltd., (Montreal, Que.), *"Depos Art"* in sterling.

Cartier, jewelry firm founded in Paris (1869) by Louis Francois Cartier; succeeded (1874) by son, Albert. In 1920's produced elite Art Deco pieces.

Christiansen, Hans, (1866-1945), German designer of brooches and pendants in silver.

Clavering, C. Napier, English jewelry designer.

Climax Mesh Bag Co., Newark, N. J., silver plated mesh.

Colonna, Edward, French jewelry designer who inspired Van de Velde and Horta; Colonna worked with Tiffany and designed jewelry for Samuel Bing's Paris Shop, *"Maison de l'Art Nouveau"*.

Cook, Thomas A., jeweler/designer of mosaics; Frenchman who worked w/Cook was Gabriel Mourney.

Cooper, John Paul, (1869-1933), British silversmith and jeweler who worked in gemstones rather than precious gems; jewelry decorated w/sculptured figures. Also worked in ivory and shagreen (a dyed leather, usually green).

Cournault, Etienne, (1891-1948), French jewelry designer and maker who worked w/Jean Despres.

Cranach, William Lucas von,German jeweler famous for *Art Nouveau* pieces.

Curtis, H. H. Co., Inc., (N. Attleboro, Mass.), German Silver bags.

Cuzner, Bernard, (1877-1956), British silversmith/jeweler who designed "Cymric" silver jewelry for Liberty & Co., c. 1900; author: "A Silversmith's Manual" (1935).

Dammouse, Albert-Louis, (1848-1926), French maker of *pate-de-verre*. (See Glossary)

Dawson, Edith (wife of Nelson), designer of "new" jewelry.

Dawson, Nelson, (1859-1942), British silversmith & jeweler, with a fine reputation for enamelling.

Debut, Jules, (1838-1900), French jewelry designer.

De Sousy, Charles, British designer of "commercial" jewelry.

Decorchemont, Francoise-Emila, (c. 1900) excelled in *pate-de-verre*.

Debois, M. Jules, French jeweler of whose designs writer, Gabriel Mourney, wrote: "...beautiful female forms in dreamy or voluptuous attitude, sleeping amid the masses of their abundant hair...".

Despres, Jean, (b. 1889-?), French goldsmith & jeweler who exhibited in the 1925, *"L'Exposition Internationale des Arts Decoratifs et Industriels Modernes";* he was an exponent of "Art Deco" at its early beginnings.

Despret, Georges, (1862-1952), Frenchman who experimented in *pate-de-verre.*

Dixon, Arthur, English jewelry designer.

Dresser, Dr. Christopher, (1834-1904), British designer who popularized Japonism in the decorative arts through his "Principles of Design", (c. 1871) wherein his articles were aimed primarily to the silversmith and jeweler.

Dufrene, Maurice, (1876-1955), a prolific designer of *art nouveau* jewelry and other decorative arts; worked for *La Maison Modern* designing jewelry (1900).

Dunand, Jean, (1877-1942), great proponent of Art Deco.

Eckmann, Otto, (1865-1902), German designer who was one of the Munich group of artists, *Jugendstil* movement (1890).

Editeur, F. V., French jeweler who executed the designs of Paul Richard and E. Becker in *chatelaines,* watches and chains; his own designs incorporated pearl drops.

Eisenloeffel, Jan, (1876-1967), Dutch jeweler who produced geometric pieces in copper, brass, and enamels; he studied w/Josef Hoffman, mainstay of *Wiener Werkstatte* (Vienna Workshop that spearheaded the Austrian modern movement). Geometric design in the aforementioned media was typical of the *Werkstatte's* output.

Epinay De Briot, Prosper (b. 1836-?), French Count who made figurative jewelry.

Ewald, Reinhold, German enamelist and jewelry designer.

Faberge', famous jewelry firm founded by Gustav Faberge' in St. Petersburg, Russia, which drew international acclaim following the recognition of jewelry work by Peter Carl Faberge', especially in the 1900 Paris Exhibition.

Fahrner, Theodor (1868-1928) jewelry firm in Pforzheim, Germany that exported wares to Murrle, Bennett & Co., (England); Fahrner belonged to Darmstadt artist's colony (1898) and exhibited in Vienna's 1st *Secession* exhibition. (Plates 3 and 33.)

Falize, Andre', (1872-1936), French jeweler.

Feuillatre, Eugene, (1870-1916), French jeweler/enameler who was a student of Lalique and worked as an enameler in Lalique's workshop before opening his own in 1899; master of *plique-a-jour* enameling on silver and platinum, he exhibited in the 1900 Paris Centennial Exhibition & the Turin Int'l Exhibition, 1902. His major works are in gold, silver and glass. (Plates 39 and 49.)

Fisher, Alexander, (1864-1936), British jeweler who worked mainly in silver and enamels; also figurative sculpture in jewelry. Best known for his exquisite enamels.

Fisher, Kate, British jewelry designer.

Follet, Paul, French jewelry designer.

Fonseque & Olive, jewelry establishment that produced a wide range of *art nouveau* designed jewelry. (French)

Foster, Theodore W. & Bros. Co., (Providence, R. I.), sterling. (Plate 47)

Fouquet, Georges, (1862-1857), French goldsmith and jeweler who produced Alphonse Mucha's designs in jewelry for actress Sarah Bernhardt. He employed designers Tourrette, Desvosiers, as well as Mucha who designed the interior of Fouquet's Parisian shop; Georges Fouquet used various colored stones, pearls, and a great deal of enameling, but primarily his creative designs of such superb artistry, put him in a category of his own.

Fouquet, Jean (b. 1899-?), son of Georges Fouquet, exhibited in the 1925 "Art Deco" exhibition; his pieces showed the effect of Cubism in design.

Frampton, George, jewelry designer from Glasgow (Scotland).

France, Georgina Cave, British designer/jeweler who worked in the "production line" of Liberty & Co., proponents of the Arts & Crafts movement in jewelry.

Frank M. Whiting & Co., Providence, R. I., jewelry mfg. (Plate 37.)

Friedmann's Nachfolger, D. & M. Lowenthal, jewelers (German), who executed designs by H. Christiansen (1866-1945).

Gaillard, Lucien (1861-?), French silversmith and jeweler who owned his own company; influenced by his visit to Japan, he used Japanese techniques of mixed metals combined with unusual gemstones, horn and ivory; experimented with shadings of silver through chemical means. Produced beautiful pieces c. 1900.

Galle, Emile, (1846-1904), French designer who inspired *Art Nouveau* artists with his work in glass, for which he's primarily known.

Gargallo, Pablo, (1881-1934), primarily a sculptor, he produced unusual jewelry in 1915-16. (Spain).

Gariod, Paris-based jewelry firm that employed L. Gautrait to design specialized jewelry of the period.

Gaskin, Arthur Joseph, (1862-1928), British silversmith and jeweler who, in 1899, designed "Cymric" silver for Liberty & Co.; specializing in enamels, he was one of those whose influence brought the Arts & Crafts movement to Birmingham, England.

Gaudi, (Barcelona), jewelry designer of the Spanish "new art".

Gautrait, L., (c. 1900), French jeweler.

Gilbert, Alfred, jewelry designer, Glasgow.

Goldsmiths' & Silversmiths' Co., (1890-1952), British manufacturers and retailers, London.

Gonzalez, Julio, (1876-1942), Spanish sculptor and goldsmith who integrated much open-work in his jewelry.

Gorham Corporation, The, (Providence, R. I., & N. Y.); jewelers c. 1815-18; 1865, set up design workshop for *art nouveau* jewelry, with designs by English silversmith, William Codman, trademarked "Martele" sterling.

Grasset, Eugene, (1841-1917), Swiss designer with a passion for Japanese art which he incorporated in his work; he designed jewelry for Vever which popularized *art nouveau* eclectic jewelry ornamentation. The Paris based firm of Vever specialized in *art nouveau* production.

Gropius, Walter, founder in main of influential *Bauhaus,* (1919), Weimer, Germany.

Gross, Karl, (b. 1869-?), German jewelry designer.

Guild of Handicraft, British guild (1888-1902), founded by C. R. Ashbee, that produced jewelry in the "new art" style.

Haseler, W. H. & Co., (1870-1927), Birmingham based manufacturers of jewelry in partnership with Liberty & Co.; also produced "Cymric" silver (1899); "Tudric" pewter (1903). (Also known as Hasler Bros. and/or W. H. Haseler & Son).

Hilman, W., Swedish jeweler.

Heaton, Clement, British jeweler and enamelist.

Hirne, French jewelry firm, (Paris), that produced designs by A. F. Thesmar.

Hodel, Prof. Joseph A., British jewelry designer.

Hodgkinson, Ethel M., British jewelry designer.

Hoffman, Josef, (1870-1955), Austrian designer whose designs were made by *Wiener Werkstatte* (1913); he was founder member of Vienna *Secession* movement (1897) and co-founder of *Wiener Werkstatte* (1903). Founded *Oesterreichische Werkbund* (1912).

Horner, Charles (Halifax based manufacturer using Chester Hallmark); English firm that pioneered *Art Nouveau* jewelry on a grand scale for mass distribution. Prized pieces, especially by hatpin collectors; primarily sterling with Celtic line, thistle-cut stones, exquisite peacock enamels. (Plates 20-23-43-51)

Iribe, Paul (d. 1935), French designer who, according to Jacques Cocteau's "Portraits Souvenir, 1900-1914", (published 1935), made jewelry designs for Lalique.

Jacquin, M., French jeweler/designer who exhibited at Paris 1900 exhibition, of whom Gabriel Mouray wrote: "...(he had) a love for natural forms. Out of a flower, a piece of seaweed, or any humble motif, vegetable or animal...", Jacquin created his *"nouveau"* jewelry.

Jensen, Georg, (1877-1935), Danish jeweler who worked in silver and opened his own jewelry shop in Copenhagen (1904), then exporting to other countries as well. (Plate 51)

Jillander, A., Danish jeweler and designer.

Johansgate, Carl, established manufacturing firm (1876) in Oslo, Norway.

Jones, Albert Edward (1879-1954), British jeweler reputed for his handmade beaten silver jewelry often decorated with turquoise.

Jones, Owen (1809-1874), designed ornamental jewelry for the masses, advocating natural forms for decorations; highly influential in future renderings of Arts & Crafts designs.

Jonest, Victor (c. 1895), New York-based jeweler that produced "French Jewelry and fancy goods".

Julius Kirschner & Co., (New York), mfg. mesh silver plated bags.

Kallert, Karl, Austrian silversmith at *Wiener Werkstatte.*

Kerr (See Wm. B. Kerr Co.)

Kielland, Valentin Axel, (1866-?), designer who made jewelry in his native Oslo, Norway.

King, Jessie Marion, (1876-1949), British jewelry designer, influenced by the Scottish "Glasgow School of Art"; specialized in designing "Cymric" jewelry for Liberty & Co.

Koehler, Florence (American), designer and jeweler.

Kurzer & Wolf, Austrian jewelers located in Vienna.

L'Orfevrerie, Christophle, (c. 1839), French silversmiths, pioneered electroplate in France and mass-produced jewelry designed by Lucien Gaillard, Eugene Colonna, George de Feure, all exponents of *art nouveau.*

LaCloche, French manufacturers and jewelers (c. 1897), who in 1920, set the fashion for jewelry pieces highly enameled, with carved stones, much in the Oriental mode.

LaFarge, John (American), exhibited decorative designs at 1900 Paris *"Exposition Universelle Internationale"*; he was much influenced by Morris' Arts and Crafts Movement in America.

La Maison Moderne, French firm that used designs by Maurice Dufrene, Paul Follot, Orazzi, etc., to produce "popular" jewelry that had quality yet was "mass-produced" to satisfy public demand for "new art" jewelry.

La Pierre Mfg. Co., (Newark, N. J.), produced sterling in "Thin Model Engraved" and "Violet" patterns. (Plate 37)

Lalique, Rene, (1860-1945), French master and innovator of "high" *Art Nouveau* forms in jewelry and glass. Lalique was apprenticed to Louis Aucoc (1876); also worked for Cartier and Boucheron jewelry firms as an independent jeweler. In 1890's, worked with glass and non-precious stones; 1895 produced first nude female figure in jewelry. Took over *Destape* workshop as his own (1885), and reopened his own shop on *Place Vendome,* Paris (1905). His entire jewelry production exhibited at the 1900 *Expositon Universelle Internationale* was purchased and is now exhibited at Gulbenkian Foundation, Lisbon, along with other ornamental jewelry, the "most spectacular *Art Nouveau* in existence". From 1881-1905, Lalique was a freelance jeweler; in 1911, he phased out of jewelry after receiving a contract to supply bottles and containers for the Paris firm of Coty (perfumes). Lalique devoted remainder of his life to glass-making which included beads and buttons in the Art Deco fashion.

Lambert, Theodore, (b. 1857-?), French jewelry designer.

Larcombe, E. (Miss), jewelry designer.

Lederer (See S. & B. Lederer, Co.)

Liberty & Co., (1875-) founded by Arthur Lasenby Liberty. This London based firm was a major force in promoting the "new art" in Britain, America, and the Continent. W. H. Haseler Co., Birmingham, manufactured for Liberty, on a mass-production basis, silver "Cymric" and pewter "Tudric" jewelry pieces in Celtic designs produced by a score of well-known designers: Archibald Knox, Arthur Gaskin, Fred Partridge, William Hutton, Edgar Simpson, Oliver Baker, Gertrude Smith, Kate Harris, Jesse M. King, J. Paul Cooper, Henry Wilson, etc.; however, most of the jewelry was made by anonymous jewelers/designers and the pieces were sold under the Liberty trademark. (Plate 46)

Lienard, Paul, (1849-1900), French jewelry designer.

Likarz, Marcia, (b. 1893-?), Austrian enamelist and designer whose work was produced at *Weiner Werkstatte.*

London & Ryder, British company of silversmiths and jewelers that produced commercial designs copied by others for mass-produced jewelry c. 1876.

Mackintoch, Charles Rennie, (1868-1928), jewelry designer and leader of the "Glasgow School" which produced the most elegant Celtic designs which influenced the Arts & Crafts Movement in both Austria and Germany. His wife, Margaret MacDonald (1865-1933) largely influenced-Mackintoch's style; both were of the "Glasgow Four" (see Glossary).

Macnair, Frances (Glasgow), jewelry designer.

Magnussen, Eric, (1884-1961), pioneer of Danish *art nouveau* who exhibited his jewelry in Copenhagen (1901); owned his own company and was a superb artist/craftsman.

Maison Vever, Paris jewelry firm employing many *art nouveau* "specialists".

Mangeant, M., French jeweler who exhibited in Paris exhibition (1900), and of whom Gabriel Mouray wrote: "...with mother-of-pearl and hammered *repousse'* silver, (he) has created charming jewels..."

Marks, Gilbert Leigh, (1861-1905), British silversmith for various manufacturers.

Masriera, Luis, (1872-1958), Spanish artisan who studied enameling techniques under Lossier (Geneva); credited in 1895 with revitalizing jewelry making both in Spain and South America.

Matthey Johnson & Co. Ltd., British company that pioneered platinum research (c. 1851); world's largest bullion firm; still makes component parts for the jewelry trade, i. e., earring clips, etc. (Founded 1817)

Mauser Mfg. Co., (Mt. Vernon Co., Silversmiths, Inc.), Mt. Vernon, N. Y., made sterling silver patterns: *L'Art Nouveau* and *"La Vision"*.

McLeish, Annie, British jewelry designer.

Mealy Mfg. Co., (Baltimore, Md.), made "hand wrought 925-1000" sterling pieces.

Michelson, A., Scandinavian jewelers in Copenhagen, founded 1841, that used designs by H. Slott-Muller.

Moore, Edward C., (d. 1891), began making jewelry designs in 1848 for Tiffany; much Oriental and Indian influence in his designs.

Morris, May, (1862-1938), daughter of Wm. Morris, who designed jewelry, but beads were her speciality. Although her father, William Morris, is largely credited with the sweeping Arts & Crafts Movement and influence, he was not involved in jewelry design, making, or manufacture; his element was furniture and textiles. A political activist, and anti-establishment, he was most vocal in protesting "machine manufacture", but toward the end of his life he made peace with the mechanical brute that had been tamed by other artisans. It was not until 1874, at the age of 40, that he first began his experiments with fabric design.

Morris, Talwin, Glasgow jewelry designer.

Moser, Koloman, (1868-1918), Austrian designer of jewelry and one of the founders of *Vienna Secession Movement* (1897); established *Vienna Werkstatte* with Hoffman and Warndorfer (1903).

Mucha, Alphonse Marie, (1860-1939), Czechoslovakian designer and decorative artist who shared a design studio with American artist, Whistler; Mucha (pronounced Moo-ka), designed fantastic jewelry for Georges Fouquet (c. 1898); produced a portfolio of designs for craftsmen: *L'Art Nouveau* and *Le Style Mucha*; highly influenced by British graphic artist, Aubrey Beardsley. Mucha's designs were copied in many of the French "high" *Art Nouveau* pieces produced by others.

Murphy, H. G., (1884-1939), British silversmith and jeweler who worked in Arts & Crafts technique until about 1920 when he adopted the Art Deco style.

Murrle, Bennet & Co., British manufacturers of gold and silver jewelry set with gems; used German as well as British designs, the former in cooperation with Theodor Fahrner, Pforzheim based jewelry firm. (Plate 43)

Navarre, Henri, (1885-1971), French jeweler who produced pieces in bizarre sculptured shapes.

Newburyport Silver Co., (Keene, New Hampshire), produced sterling pieces in following patterns: "New Art", "Pond Lily and Nymph" and "Maiden Hair".

Nics Brothers, metalworkers who made Art Deco jewelry.

Nienhuis, Bert, (1873-1960), Dutch designer of jewelry in the *"Jugendstil"* style prior to 1908.

Nilsson, Wiwen, Swedish jeweler in Art Deco fashion.

O'Donnel, J. R., American firm, (Newark, N. J.), specializing as supplier of enamel paintings; marking O'D or O'DNL.

Olbrich, Josef Maria, (1867-1908), German jewelry designer who founded the artists colony at Darmstadt and founding member of the *Vienna Secession* (1897).

Parks, George, (Geo. W. Parks Co., Providence, R. I.), made silver-plated wares with patterns: "Aurora", "Lily-of-the-Valley", "Lotus", "Oriental" and "Titania".

Partridge, Fred, T., British jeweler.

Peche, Dagobert, (1887-1923) Austrian active in *Wiener Werkstatte*; created rich ornamental style which influenced others.

Perchin, Michael Evlampievich, (b. 1860-?), leading artisan jeweler for House of Faberge; made *Art Nouveau* designed Easter eggs, most famous is fabulous Lily-of-the-Valley.

Pickett, Edith, British jewelry designer.

Pflaumer, Eugen, German jeweler who worked at Gablonz, (Czech.) prior to 1914; a master goldsmith he was also active in the *Wiener Werkstatte* in early 20th Century.

Prouve, Victor Emile, (1859-1943), French designer of jewelry who worked and studied with Emile Galle; also Director of *Ecole des Beaux Arts* (Nancy, France).

Prutscher, Otto, (1880-1949), Austrian designer and member of *Weiner Werkstatte*.

Ramsden, O., British designer of "commercial" jewelry.

Rasummy, F., designer and maker of jewelry.

Rathbone, Richard, British designer of "commercial" jewelry.

Rault, Louis, (1847-1903), French jeweler.

Rickets, Charles, Glasgow designer of jeweler for "masses".

Rico, F., British jewelry designer.

Rivaud, Charles, French jewelry designer.

Robert, Rene, (1893-?) French jeweler who won a gold medal for his Art Deco showing at the Paris 1925 exhibition.

Robinson, Edith, British jeweler/designer who did fine enamels on silver jewelry; wife of Nelson Dawson.

Rhode, Johan, (1856-1935), Danish designer/jeweler who collaborated with Georg Jensen in silverworks and jewelry (c. 1909).

S. & B. Lederer & Co., Providence, R. I. based jewelry manufacturer who used a star as trademark. (Plate 24)

Samuel C. Jackson's Son, New York firm manufacturing jewelry cases.

Saint-Yves, French arts and crafts designer who worked for *La Maison Moderne* creating jewelry.

Sandoz, Gerard, (b. 1902-?), exhibited jewelry in 1925 Art Deco Exhibition, Paris.

Scheidt, Georg Adam, Austrian jeweler, silversmith and enameler (c. 1900).

Scher, A., jewelry maker/designer.

Schneckendorf, Josef Emil, (1865-1949), German jeweler who utilized glass in his work.

Sedding, G. E., British designer/maker, Arts & Crafts.

Serriere, Jean, metalworker who made Art Deco jewelry.

Silver, Reginald (Rex), British designer for Liberty & Co., "Cymric" jewelry.

Simpson, Edgar, British jewelry designer/maker who exhibited jewelry in Vienna *Secessionist* Exhibitions (16th & 24th), showing great influence of Ashbee's work.

Simpson, Hall, Miller & Co., (Wallingford, Conn.), made silver plate in patterns: "Les Saisons" and "Mikado".

Spence, Isabel, Scottish designer of jewelry and member of Glasgow School of Art.

Stabler, Harold, (1872-1945), British designer of silver and enamels.

Sunyer, Ramon, Spanish jeweler who exhibited jewelry in Paris 1912 and 1925 exhibits, taking a gold medal in latter; came from family of jewelers established 1835.

Traquair, Phoebe, British designer of "commercial" jewelry.

Templier, M. Paul, French jeweler who worked in monochrome metals (reddish or greenish) from designs of M. Theodore Lambert.

Templier, Raymond, (1891-?) artist, jeweler, designer and Art Deco proponent since 1911.

Thesmar, Andre-Fernand, (1843-1912), French enamelist who specialized in *plique-a-jour* enamels in jewelry as well as Japanese inspired designs in *cloisonne*.

Tiffany & Co., Inc., founded 1812 (New York); mfg. jewelry (1848). (See Louis Comfort Tiffany)

Tiffany, Louis Comfort, son of founder of Tiffany & Co., Inc. (New York), founded "The Studio Workshop" where his designs and experiments in glass influenced jewelry design (c. 1902); his work was greatly influenced by Persian, Japanese, and "Aesthetic Period" arts; produced few *art nouveau* jewelry pieces and none for "the masses". Adapted Byzantine motifs and colors in earlier *art nouveau* forms; then Lalique's influence introduced symbolism mixed with eclectic patterns in some pieces of jewelry.

Unger Bros., (Newark, N. J.), prolific producers of *Art Nouveau* jewelry in silver; by 1915, 35 patterns were discontinued: *"Art Nouveau"*, "Bride-of-the-Wave", "Water Lily", *"Secrete Des Fleurs"*. "Man-in-Moon", "Maiden Hair Fern", etc. (Plates 3-33-51-110)

Van Den Eersten & Hofmeijer, Amsterdam-based jewelers and silversmiths.

Van De Velde, Henry Clemens, (1863-1957), Belgian designer of jewelry whose style was the foundation for jewelry manufacture at Theodor Fahrner factory, (Pforzehim, Germany). He also designed interior of S. Bing's *"Art Nouveau"* shop in Paris. Belgium proponent of Arts & Crafts Movement.

Valenti, Juan, (1886-1958), Spanish manufacturer and retail jeweler, leader in trade in early 1900's.

Veazey, David, British jewelry designer.

Verneuil, Maurice Pillard, (1869-?), French designer who published books on European and Oriental design and ornament.

Vernier, Seraphin Emile, (1852-1927), French goldsmith using Egyptian motifs in jewelry.

Vever, French jewelry firm founded in Metz (1821), moved to Paris (1871). Paul Vever (1851-1915) and Henri Vever (1854-1942), were among leading *Art Nouveau* jewelers, working from many designs by E. Grasset.

Vever, Henri, (1854-1942), (see above).

Vogt, A., German firm of metalworkers and jewelers at Pforzheim that executed enamels after designs by H. Christiansen and others.

Von Cranach, Wilhelm Lucas (1861-1918), German designer and jewelry maker working in gold and in figurative style.

Werner, O. M., (c. 1900), jeweler/designer w/firm J. H. Werner, court jewelers.

Whiting, Frank M. (Frank M. Whiting & Co.), manufactured sterling jewelry in N. Attleboro, Mass. (Plate 37)

Whiting Manufacturing Co. (1866-1905), silversmiths and jewelers, Newark, N. J., who produced pieces inspired by Japanese decoration.

Whiting Mfg. Co., (Bridgeport, Conn.), manufactured sterling jewelry.

Wiener Werkstatte, Vienna workshop that produced wide range of jewelry designed J. Hoffman, K. Moser, D. Peche, E. Wimmer, etc.

Wilson, Henry J., (1864-1934), leading designer/jeweler who worked in London (1896), Paris (1902), and traveled to Italy and the United States bringing Arts and Crafts Movement influence with him.

Win, R., British jewelry designer.

Wm. B. Kerr Co., (Newark, N. J.), producer of large amounts of *Art Nouveau* sterling jewelry, among patterns: "Floradora", "*La Paris*" (Plate 37)

Wm. Link Co., (Newark, N. J.), producer of sterling jewelry.

Wolfers, Philippe, (1858-1929), Belgium goldsmith and jeweler (Brussels), who in 1895 turned to the "new art"; produced pieces w/floral and insect motifs in gold; 1897, incorporated ivory from the Belgium Congo in his work. By 1900, his designs became more symmetrical and abstract; 1925 exhibited pieces w/geometrical patterned "lace" designs at the 1925, *Arts Decoratif* style exhibition, (Art Deco), Paris.

Woodside Sterling Co., (New York), produced sterling pieces in patterns: "Butterfly Girl", "Iris", "*La France*", "*Tokio*", among others.

Zimpel, Julius, (1896-1925), Austrian designer of jewelry for *Wiener Werkstatte.*

CHAPTER II
GLOSSARY OF JEWELRY TERMS AND TYPES, INCLUDING PRONUNCIATION

Abalone *(ab-a-lō-ñē)* - Pacific Coast sea-shell w/lining of gray/pink pearlized substance.

Accessories - Jeweled accessories played a prominent part in the late 19th and 20th Century costume. They held the unique position of being useful jewelry, combining beauty and utility. The useful articles included the memorandum tablet, the *lorgnette*, the *chatelaine*, buckles, hatpins, fashionable fans, pocket opera glasses, buckles, sash pins, and various beaded bags and purses. The *chatelaines* were equipped with several chains to accommodate the following "necessaries": coin purses, vanity cases in the form of lockets for powder puffs and mirrors, silver card cases, a pencil, a place for lip salve, *vinaigrettes*, a bon bon box for scent pills, and a tiny writing tablet. These accessories added an intangible expression of charm to the individual costume. The Art Deco period (circa 1925), brought the powder and rouge compact, lipstick, and cigarette holder for the more "free-minded" woman.

Agate - A variety of quartz or natural gemstone, the most common being the banded or striped agate. Among the varieties of quartz known as agate, is black onyx often used for cameos and *intaglios*. The carnelian or red agate is prized for beads and *intaglio* seals. Moss-colored agate or gray-striped agate from Scotland was very popular during Victorian times while Brazilian agates and those mined in India contributed to requirements for mass-produced jewelry in the late 19th and 20th centuries.

Aigrette *(ā´gret)* - A hair ornament with a plume or spray most often accentuated by either a jewel or buckle. Buckles and clasps were ingenious works of *art nouveau* and deco jewelers.

Alloy - Combination of metals fused together. A base metal mixed with a precious ore to make it workable, to harden it, or to change its color.

Amber - A yellowish-brown fossil resin. This fossilized resin, also found in black and varieties of brown and orange, comes from ancient forests of fir trees or mined from under the Baltic Sea. The orange color amber comes from Italy.

Amethyst - A gemstone in shades from pale lavender to deep purple found in Russia, Brazil, Uruguay, Ceylon, and the United States. (Plates 27-30-50)

Arabesque *(ăr 'ăb-esk)-* Flowing scrollwork in line, leaves, curlicues, etc., often in low relief.

Art Deco (circa 1925) - A stilted, stylized design, a transition from *art nouveau* which found its influence in the 1925 *Exposition Internationale des Arts Decoratifs,* (Paris), as well as in the art of Africa, the American Indian, ancient Egypt, Greek and Roman architecture, and proponents of Cubism and Dadism.

Art Nouveau *(art-nu-vō)* - Designs in jewelry which incorporate undulating curves, spirals, and flowing lines, and especially the use of the female form as introduced by Rene Lalique, master of "high" *art nouveau* jewelry. The influence of Japanese art forms is also most apparent, popularized by the 1876 trade between Japan and the Continent as well as earlier Oriental art and wares exhibits (1854). *Art Nouveau* derives its title from Samuel Bing's Paris Shop, *Galeries de l'Art Nouveau,* (1895). In its various interpretations, it was known as:

America: *Art Nouveau*

England: *Art Nouveau* or *Morris Style*

France: *l'Art Nouveau, Style 1900,* or *Le Style Moderne*

Austria and Czechoslovakia: *Recession, Secession,* or *Sezession.*

Belgium: *Les Vinget,* (Brussels), for the 20 proponents of the "new art", or *l'Art Nouveau.*

Germany (or German speaking countries): *Jugenstil,* after the magazine, *Jugend,* meaning "youth" or "new born". (In Germany, sometimes *Lilien Stil)*

Holland: *Stijl*

Italy: *Stile Liberty,* after London's Liberty & Co., the Regent Street department store, featuring "modern" merchandise.

Spain: *Arte Joven,* meaning "young art".

131

Bags (see PURSES)

Baguette - A narrow rectangular-cut stone most often chosen for diamonds. The *baguette*-cut was influenced by the interest in Cubism of the 1920's. When associated with emeralds it is called "emerald-cut".

Bakelite - A trade-mark for a synthetic resin chemically formulated and named after Belgian chemist, L. H. Backeland, (1909). It is for molding items formerly created in Celluloid or hard rubber. Bakelite is opaque. It was capable of being molded and carved, and some *art nouveau* and deco jewelry were crafted in Bakelite; but the greatest innovators were the Art Deco and "Moderne" jewelry designers of the 30's and the 40's. (Plate 2)

Basse-Taille *(bass-a-tie)* - Metal plate cut to various depths into which translucent enamel is poured, thus achieving a 3-dimensional effect. The depth of relief produces shadings from light to dark. The deeper the metal is cut, the darker the color; where shallow routing occurs, the shading is almost transparent. This routing is worked *intaglio*, the opposite of *repousse*. (Plates 4-14-43)

Bead - An ornament with a hole end to end into which a needle can be inserted. Most glass beads came from Czechoslovakian, Italian, and American glass-blowing factories. However, Rene'Lalique is known to have made and sold beads through his catalogue and shop. Beads are made from gemstones, metals, shells, seeds, ivory, bone, stone, and horn. Glass beads are made on a blowing rod and then pierced.

Bezel - A groove or flange which holds a stone secure in its setting. (Plate 27)

Belts - Metal belts, often made in solid gold, were used to accentuate a small waist. The chasing and engraving on the metal was executed so as to pick up the pattern of the lace on the garment being worn. The buckles often were designed with *art nouveau* and art deco motifs.

Bijouterie *(be-zhoo t-re)* - Jewelers working in media of metals, usually gold and silver, as opposed to gem-setting. Metals are worked to produce elegant pieces and "trinkets of virtue".

Birthstone Jewelry (see GEMS)

Black Glass Jewelry - Imitation jet or onyx. The finest black glass was made in Jablonec district of Czechoslovakia. (Plate 44)

Blister Pearl - Irregularly-shaped pearly deposit in oyster which is sometimes hollow as opposed to *baroque* pearl which is a *solid* irregular shaped pearl.

Box Setting - A stone enclosed in a box-shaped setting with edges of metal pressed down to hold it in place.

Bracelets - Bracelets have been popular since time immemorial. *Art nouveau* and deco jewelers produced "jointed" wide-cuffed bracelets and unjointed bangle-type bracelets, the latter often given in friendship. Adjustable bracelets were worn by both ladies and infants and had an adjustable "expando" mechanism. Because Queen Victoria's Prince Consort presented her with a wedding ring in the form of two serpents entwining, bracelets with this motif were very much in voque during her long reign. With the discovery of King Tut's tomb, the serpent again became a symbol in many pieces of jewelry, and most eloquently in the bracelets of the *nouveau* and *deco* eras. The bangle bracelet was originally called a "bangle ring" although it was made to fit around the wrist. It resembled an enlarged ring and was called a "bangle ring", because the wire was very narrow and resembled a wedding band. The adjustable cuff or band bracelet was another innovation of the 1890's, as was the coil or mesh wire bracelet available in gold plate or rolled gold. The coil bracelets were adjustable in that being a coil, they could be stretched. The "wedding band" type of bracelet could also be expanded with either end separating and then popping together after it was placed on the wrist. From 1850 to 1910 the "stiff band" or cuff bracelet was preferred and was from 1" to 2" wide. High relief and much *niello* (black tracery enamel work) were featured on the cuff bracelets.

Brass - Yellowish-gold color which is primarily an alloy of copper, tin, zinc, or other base metal. This metal is the base for much gilded or gold-washed jewelry of the *art nouveau* and art deco periods.

Brilliants - Another term for paste, *strass*, or rhinestones.

Brooch (see PINS)

Buckles - Buckles were wrought for belts, cummerbunds, sashes, shoes, capes, and hats. Some belt buckles were actually brooches with simulated hasps. (Plate 8) The buckle was pinned in front of a sash, belt, cummerbund, or hat. Buckles were finished in Roman gold, rose gold, antique gold, silver, French grey, oxidized metals, and in gun metal. They were most fashionable after the turn-of-the-century. When the belt buckle was designed to meet at an angle, rather than in a horizontal manner, it was called the "new dip" belt buckle. Shirtwaists were "in" at this same period and women demanded buckles that matched pins, studs, as well as hatpins and collar stays. Colonial-type shoe buckles came in oxidized silver and were used to accent a brown or black calfskin pump with a very high tongue. The clasp of the tongue fit into the colonial buckle, and the shoe was called "Colonial Pump" because this type buckle was a reproduction of the earlier fashion. Many colonial-type shoe buckles were of beautiful cut steel. (Plate 48) The color of the metal, called "French Grey", often had hand-etching, and was usually square. However, this soon gave way to many new shapes, particularly the oblong. In the 1915-25 era there was a new color called "brown jewelry" which was a kind of seal-brown tone of metal and went very well with the popular brown fabric which was becoming the vogue at the beginning of the 20th Century. With the demise of Queen Victoria, brown had come into fashion as well as French Grey. In the second decade of the 20th Century, the sash buckle with the simulated hasp was introduced on the wider cummerbund-type belts which were worn closer to the hips rather than to the waist, a fashion note of the deco period. During the reign of Empress Eugenie (France), belts at the waistline were very much in vogue. The Empress had a beautiful figure and naturally wanted to accentuate her very small waistline. Small waists were in until after WWI when the flapper girl costume brought the so-called "waistline" to well below the curve of the hip. (Plates 14-20-23-50)

Buttons, (Dress) - Some dress buttons came in sets of three and were joined by a very delicate lovely link chain which prevented loss. The stud end was worn inside the blouse which, before 1900, was called a "waist". The waist was called a "shirt" from 1900 to 1920 and then a "blouse". Dress buttons were beautifully engraved, enameled, with raised borders, and some were set with garnets, pearls, or turquoise. The same sets of dress buttons were made in miniature for children's wear. The children's buttons were much more simple in design, with a ribbed or polished front, occasionally accented with a very small half-pearl or garnet. Children's and women's dress buttons came in many shapes: bar shape, oblong shape, and oval shape. Others had beautiful curved designs wonderfully engraved with lovely rippled or ribbed cable patterns, and were made of both natural and man-made materials. Most were die-stamped, but others were hand-crafted. (Plates 23-40)

Cabochon *(kà-bō-shón)* - A stone without facets, shaped like a dome. (Plate 30)

Cairngorm *(kâm-gorm)* -Yellow or smokey brown clear quartz mined especially in Cairngorm, Scotland, and featured in Scottish brooches and jeweled accessories.

Cage (see Mountings)

Cameo - Usually a conch shell carved in relief, depicting a scene or portrait; onyx, ivory, coral and gems were also used, as well as woods. Cameos can be molded in glass and synthetics, but natural elements *cannot be molded*. (Plate 41)

Carbuncle - A garnet gem that has been cabachon-cut.

Carat (English) or Karat (American) - Standard unit of weight for gems, or a measure for gold tabled at 1/24th part of pure gold in an alloy.

The term "Carat" is a symbol for unit weight of gems and gemstones (ct.) 1 ct. diamond = 1 ct.

The symbol "K" used for gold: 24K = 18 parts gold to 6 parts alloy, and so forth down the scale.

Carat marks began about 1890. European carat marks were: 9, 15, or 18. American jewelry was primarily 14 karat, but American and Canadian used 12K and 18K also.

10 carat gold was used for less expensive pieces and for the earlier Victorian pieces which were made before stringent hallmarking was in effect.

Carnelian (also called Cornelian) - A variety of chalcedony with a wax-like luster. A precious stone found mainly in Greece or in Asia Minor, carnelian has a translucent color which may be deep red, flesh red, or reddish-white color. It takes a good polish and cut and is ideal for seals and *intaglios*. (Plate 19)

Cartouche *(kär-tōōsh)* - A shield or scroll with curved edges used particularly on silver for monogram, crest, or initial.

Celluloid - A trade-mark of Hyatt Bros., Newark, N.J. (1868). It is a composition mainly of guncotton and camphor, resembling ivory in texture and color. It is also dyed to imitate coral, tortoise-shell, amber, malachite, etc. Originally called xylonite, Celluloid is the word most often used to cover any imitation ivory, bone, or tortoise. But there were many other imitators such as: "ivorine", "French ivory", "tortine", and the like. Celluloid should not be confused with the harder and more resiliant plastic known as Bakelite. Celluloid, being highly flammable, lost favor to phenolic resins, plastics of the 1930's. Celluloid was first used as synthetic ivory in the manufacture of billiard balls. (Plate 31)

Celtic Design - Primarily junctured lines and discs affiliated w/the ancient Celtic Cross. Denoting ancient Gaulic, British, Irish Scotch, Welsh design.

Chains - Probably the most widely used chain is the ordinary neck chain with a clasp to attach a pendant, watch, locket, medallion, etc. When Queen Victoria married Prince Albert in 1849, immediately there was a chain named for him--the "Albert Chain"--which had a lapel bar on one end and swivel or tongue-pin on the other, and was worn draped across the vest. At the center of this chain was a small jump ring which accomodated a small fob-type medallion or charm. A woman's chain of the same period was similar to the Albert Chain but much shorter and was called the "Victoria" or "Queen Chain." It usually had several charms dangling from various interruptions in the linkage. Vest chains were made mostly in solid gold, or in either 10-carat or 14-carat with a great variety of linkages. There were square, oval, flat, square twist, and ship's cable, among many others. The vest chain was popularized by the visit of Charles Dickens to this country and eventually showed up in the 1893 catalogues under "Dickens Vest Chain". Men wore their vest chains slung across the front of their vests, and women's "vest chains" were smaller duplicates of the men's chains except that they were more intricately and more delicately wrought than a man's. The woman's vest chain differed in that they had slides which shortened or tightened the chain which was then draped into a belt or pinned to the waist-shirt.

Neck chains for women could average as long as 48", but always included a slide which would keep the chain from slipping off the shoulder or looping a breast. (Plate 28) There were many neck chains, some in 10 carat or 14 carat gold. The usual length of a neck chain was from 12" to 13½". Manufactured in various lengths, they came in twisted wire, woven wire, plain link chains, barrel links, chased wire, and flat links. These neck chains (or "necklaces" as they were sometimes called), were used to accommodate small charms or pendants. The links on the chains varied from square, round, and octagon-shape, all with chased wire or extremely fancy linkage.

136

Chalcedony *(kăl-sĕd´ô-nĭ)* - A variety of quartz found in Asia Minor, primarily Greece, which has a translucent quality. The term chalcedony denotes a grayish or milky-colored quartz, such as: onyx, agate, sard, cat's eye, jasper, carnelian and chrysoprase. All take high polish and are suitable for good *intaglio* work except for the cat's eye which is polished into a carbochon-cut stone.

Champleve *(shămp´lĕ-vă)* - An enameling technique in which areas of metal are cut, etched, or routed and filled with enamel. Unlike *cloisonne*, the cells are cut rather than formed by wires. *Champleve* is most commonly applied to copper or bronze. The metals are gilded on exposed and visible surfaces. (Plates 4-14-40-43)

Channel Setting - A series of stones set close together in a straight line with the sides of the mounting gripping the outer edges of the stone.

Charms - Most charms were of low carat or gold plate. Many were set with assorted colored stones, not necessarily genuine gems. Very often charms were designed as lockets. Some could open; others had fronts that could slide out to reveal a picture of a loved one.

Around 1893 some charms were actually made of solid aluminum and were guaranteed not to tarnish or corrode. They were advertised as "...¼ the weight of silver, five times stronger than gold". There's not doubt that these aluminum charms, which were not hollow, could well be mistaken for silver. They were probably not as desirous as silver or sterling charms, but they represented a beautiful craft. The Arts and Crafts Movement experimented with lessor metals and preferred silver color to gold.

Chasing - The ornamentation of metal with grooves or lines with the use of hand-chisels and hammers. Obverse (front) chasing is called *intaglio*; chasing from reverse side, (back) is called *repousse*.

Chinoiserie *(shē nwà/z´-rē)* - Decoration or ornamentation "in the Chinese manner".

Choker - A single-strand necklace or ribbon which fits snugly around the throat. The single strand could be made of pearls, gems, or beads, but could also consist of several strands of metallic chain accentuated by a central brooch. The ribbon-type choker was made of grosgrain or velvet. To this ribbon was added a brooch, either center or off-center, determined by the particular taste of the wearer.

137

Chrome (also called Chromium) - The word comes from the Greek "chroma" which means color. Chrome is a metal that forms very hard steel-gray masses which gleam a silver color. Less than 3% mixture of chromium to steel produces an extremely hard alloy; it is used for plating base metals that easily corrode. It receives its name from the green, orange, yellow, red etc., colors which emanate from the oxide and acid which contacts specific minerals and yields a chrome-green, chrome-yellow, and other color pigments. Chrome-plated jewelry is not common since it was an experimental metal proving to be more expensive than silver-color platings. One may occasionally come upon a chrome and plastic brooch or bracelet from the Art Deco or *Art Moderne* Periods.

Chrysoprase *(krĭs-ō-prāz)-* Apple-green in color, it is actually a dyed chalcedony or agate which has a cloud-like rather than brilliant color. It is almost like "vasoline" glass, seemingly with an oily surface. This stone was very popular in *Art Nouveau* and Art Deco Periods. (Plates 19-44)

Cinnabar - Cinnabar is the only important ore of Mercury and is a brilliant red or vermillion-color mineral used as a red pigment. Most popular in China, the origin of the word is probably Chinese, as the color is sometimes referred to as "dragon's blood". The pigment is highly prized by Chinese artisans for dying in-lay work for jewelry and other artifacts.

Citrine - A pale lemon-colored gemstone of the quartz variety often mistaken for topaz.

Clasps - The "push-in" type clasp is the oldest form of clasp on bracelet or necklace. Brooch clasps had simple hooks under which a pin-shank was held in place. Eventually, safety-type devices were added. The "ball-catch" safety type of clasp consists of a ¾ circle with a small lever-type tab which completes the round and securely locks the brooch pin. This "ball-catch" was innovated in the year 1911.

A "spring-ring" clasp is in the shape of a tiny circle with a push-pin on a spring which opens and springs shut for closure of a necklace or a bracelet. This is the most common type of clasp device.

Clasps with a chain-and-pin safety feature were worn prior to 1890, while the safety clasp mentioned above was in use after the turn-of-the-century.

Ornamental clasps were worn until the 1930's, and then came the simple, screw-barrel type, followed by a chain with an open "fish hook."

Prior to die-stamped jewelry, and again in the 1930's, clasps were usually incorporated in the overall design of necklaces, pendants, chains, chokers, and bracelets. All finer designed, more expensive pieces, have such clasps. (Plate 33)

Claw-set - Tiny claws or prongs curved to hold down a stone in its mounting.

Cloisonne *(kloi´zō-nā)* - Enameling in which thin wire (silver, gold, bronze, or copper which is then gilded), is bent to form cells, *(cloisons)* and then filled with enamel. Each color is in a separate compartment, each compartment separated by thin wire. (Plate 50)

Collar Buttons & Studs - Collar buttons were made stronger and more durable than shirt studs. That is because the collar button had to fasten the collar tightly around the throat, and collars being heavily starched, they required a strong and durable fastening.

Parks Brothers & Rogers, (Providence, R. I.), were makers of the "Parkroger", "the original...one-piece collar button, stud and solderless cuff buttons...the original American Lever and Pointer collar buttons".

We think of the collar button as a very simple, round shape, but it actually came in various shapes and designs; some folded forward, some were designed with Masonic symbols, some were in a pointed shape, the point often set with a pearl or diamond.

Collar buttons came with a long or short shank and many of them had patented clamps to keep them from being lost or from loosening. Some of the patented clamps opened on a small spring and had meshing teeth on either side to secure the collar.

The collar button was not only a man's accessory but a lady's as well. Ladies' collar buttons were worn in combination sets which included the collar button, dress buttons, and cuff buttons, The collar button, usually associated with men's wear, won popularity with the shirtwaist which complemented the "Gibson Girl" attire. Women in America took on the fashionable, masculine accessory of collar buttons, cuff buttons, and dress buttons, in matching sets, usually of rolled plate, gold or silver. All were engraved or highly chased with much raised edgework.

Dress buttons were to women what dress studs were to men. Studs were worn in front of the shirt and they were highly decorative. Shirt studs were commonly worn before the turn-of-the-century and even into the late '20's. Today, shirt studs are usually associated with the tuxedo-front. (Plate 8)

Cocktail Ring - A ring produced during the Deco epoch which was weighty in design. The ring was worn at cocktail parties, dinner and after-theatre parties during the late twenties. (Plate 44)

Combs - Combs did not become purely ornamental until about 1880. Before that time they were not only decorative but functional. In the mid-'20's, the "Gibson Girl" hairdo was popular and the comb again became functional.

From 1880 to approximately 1920, the hair was arranged so as to present an attractive appearance from every viewpoint. Therefore, there was an abundance of combs, clasps, barretts, ribbons, etc., all at one time. No fashionable woman considered her wardrobe complete without a myriad of combs: side, pompadour, back and decorative. Combs were required for various coiffures such as the Greek knot or Grecian knot which was a plain coil twisted or rolled low on the neck. This type of hairdo required hairpins as well as several fancy combs which were inserted for both utility and attractiveness.

Early combs were generally made of real tortoise-shell, bone, sterling, gold, and silver. After 1900, imitation materials were more popularly used, especially in America. Back combs usually had three or more teeth and often the crest of the comb was hinged so as to be more easily inserted and more comfortable for wearing. Fancy combs were set with brilliants and Bohemian garnets, the latter being the most desirable. Imitation tortoise shell and ivory combs came under many trademarks: *NuHorn, Tuf-E-Nuf,* and *Stag,* (manufactured 1915), by Noyes Comb Co., Binghamton, N. Y. Imitation tortoise-shell combs were manufactured by Schrader & Ehlers, N. Y., who made the "Olive Dore Combs". Sadler Bros., So. Attleboro, Mass., produced the real article of tortoise-shell as did the Wagner Comb Co. of New York. The most artful combs were imported from the Continent. (Plates 15-31-45)

Conceits - A word which is used to represent curiously contrived and fanciful jewelry, or a jewelers artifice, or jeweled accessories which are quaint, artificial, or have an affected conception which flatters one's vanity. To be "plumed with conceit..",signifies an awareness or an eccentricity of dress.

The "Delineator" (March 1900) reported a "new high fashion" at the beginning of the century, stating that "dainty neck conceits" were becoming an important item in women's wardrobes.

"...there is no bit of finery so truly feminine or possessing so many charming possiblities as the tie or collar of ribbon, velvet, chiffon or lace...".

Each of these "neck conceits" was finally fastened with an unusual and attractive brooch.

Another neck conceit was a close-fitting "stock", a wide velvet ribbon folded around a stiffened foundation. Fastened on the side of the velvet ribbon was a jeweled ornament. The actual fastening of the ribbon was to the back, but the jewel pinned at the front gave the impresson that the jewel was the clasp, The neckwear of the turn-of-the-century could change a blouse or shirtwaist into varied costumes to be worn with the close-fitting skirts of the period. The waistline of the skirt was accentuated with a small jeweled clasp and often that clasp would match the brooch worn at the neck or at the shoulder.

Millinery for all seasons was given brilliancy by some of the more elaborate creations and conceits of jewels such as dull gold enameling in colored alloys, crystal carbochons, wide buckles of gold, cut steel, and rhinestones. Added to all this was the ever-popular and necessary requirement, the hatpin(s).

The parasol was a summer-time must, many of them fascinating to see as they carried out the decoration of the smartest gowns. The handles were works of art and varied greatly in length and design. A golf-lover might have a parasol-handle in the form of a putter, wrought in gun metal; an automobile ornamentation, perhaps suggesting the make of a car, or the spokes of the wheel, could serve as the ornamental handle of another umbrella. There was no end to the designs of umbrella handles for the "sportin' woman".

One of the more unusual conceits carried by men was the physician's thermometer case which was of fine quality gold. There was a chain and pen hooked to the end piece which had a socket for storage of the glass thermometer. It was ornately and beautifully engraved and very often had the insignia of the *caduceus*, signifying the medical profession. This signet was comprised of a staff or wand of Hermes/Mercury, the messenger of the gods, fabled to have two serpents coiled around him. This type case was also executed in sterling silver.

Other "conceits" consisted of infants' and children's Bib Pins which usually measured from ½" to ¾" and about 1/8" to ¼" wide, generally of gold with enameling. The word "baby", "love", or the name of the infant or child was engraved. Another novelty conceit for children was the decorative animal pin to be worn on the lapel so the joints of the animal were rendered movable. Most were wrought in sterling silver and had a pin similar to a stickpin which was then thrust into the lapel. When the pin was worn, it moved in a life-like manner. One of the more popular of this type was the *chamelion* pin.

Several 1895 catalogues offered the following jeweled conceits: sterling encased mustache combs, ladies' hat band buckles, sterling silver hat marks, folding pocket combs, key rings, umbrella straps, bag or trunk checks, armlets or garters, and glove buttoners--all in beautifully engraved sterling silver. Silver was popularized by the Arts and Crafts Movement in England.

Crystal - A colorless quartz most often implemented in cut and faceted beads, pendants, and rings. Crystal, in its natural form, is not to be confused with man-made glass.

Czechoslovakian "sunray" crystals were set into silver or gold filigree as pendants, bracelets, rings, and earrings. In the center of the "sun" was a small set consisting of a half-pearl or diamond ordinarily outlined in a tiny filigree frame.

Frosted rock crystal was utilized in both *Nouveau* and Deco jewelry.

"Cymric" - Trade name of Liberty & Company, (founded by Arthur Lasenby Liberty in 1875), under which mass-produced English Arts and Crafts designs were manufactured for the mass-market.

Cut Steel (also see Marcasite) - Metal often mistaken for marcasite. Cut steel was faceted and hand-riveted to buckle and brooch frames. Cut and faceted steel beads were used as separators or decorative accents on cloth. Some cut steel was machine-made and appeared as strips or casements rather than individual sets. (Plate 48)

Diamonds - A valuable gem of extreme hardness consisting of pure carbon. Usually clear and colorless, diamonds are sometimes yellow, blue, green, or black.

From 1850-1900, the old mine-cut diamonds were in vogue. The "brilliant-cut" has 59 or more facets and relates to more modern faceting which became popular after 1918. In 1922 the *baguette* and emerald-cut for diamonds was introduced. *Pave'*-set is probably the oldest form of setting for these gems, popularized again during the Art Deco period. (See *PAVE*-SET)

Die Stamping - To cut a design into metal for mass-production and reproduction. This superseded hand-wrought and custom-made jewelry pieces.

Depose (dē-pōz′) - A French word similar to the U. S. "copyright" or "patent".

Dragon's Breath - Simulated Mexican fire opals, made of glass, popular from 1910-1930.

Earrings - Earrings are rather easily dated: the earliest were lightweight, hollow gold, and were made with wire hooks which went through pierced ear lobes. Wire posts were popular after 1900. (Plates 5-16-19-21)

Screw-backs and ear clips were introduced at the turn-of-the-century.

Fancy "pierceless' eardrops gained popularity by 1930. Prior to this time, most women wore pierced earrings, primarily studs and/or short drops.

Edwardian Era (1901-1910) - The reign of Edward VII, which departed from Victorianism into an opulent, elegant period which was contrasted by a challenge to social values, mores, and political change. Elegance in costume witnessed millinery magic, resulting in the "glory" of the hatpin. It was also the period of the greatest innovations of "high" *Art Nouveau,* jewelry.

Electroplating (or Electro-Plating) - The plating is achieved by immersing the jewelry into an electro-magnetic acid bath which deposits a thin layer of gold, silver, or other metal onto a lesser metal.

Emerald - Commonly dark-green color, it is also found in varied shades of green. An "emerald-cut" stone is oblong or square-cut and is the usual cutting for a genuine emerald. Emerald-cut was introduced in the 1920's with the vital interest in Cubism.

Enamel (also see Bâsse-Taille, Champleve´, Cloisonne, Limoges, Niello, and Plique´-A-Jour) - Enameling is a firing of melted glass. The powdered glass mixture is composed of feldspar, quartz, soda, borax, calcium phosphates and kaolin. Metallic oxides produce the various desired colors. There is little transparent, clear, see-through, colorless enameling; "translucent" is a more definitive term. But the word "transparent" has been an accepted term for *plique´-a-jour* enameling which permits light to pass through as in stained glass.

Engraving - Cutting lines into metal which are either decorative or symbolic. Method used in monogramming a crest, *cartouche,* or escutcheon.

Escutcheon *(es-kŭch-ŭn)* - Small metal plate used atop an ornament or ring for monogram or signet.

Facet - Small flat surface cut into gemstone, glass, or shell. Purpose is to refract light or enhance design.

Festoon - A garland of chain or chains decorated with ornamental drops or pendants which lay on a curve against a woman's upper bosom, or draped across a man's chest. A *chatelaine* chain could well be worn in festoon fashion, meaning it would be draped from shoulder to shoulder, forming a curve at the center fall.

Filigree - To apply thread-like wire and decorate into a lace, lattice, or cobweb network. (Plate 44)

Fin´ de Siecle *(fin´dē sēal)* - (French), "end-of-the-century". Expression in art, fashion, society, and jewelry, denoting "decadence" or restlessness; daring, *avant garde*.

Findings - Metal parts used by jewelers for finishing an ornament.

Fleur-de-Lis´ *(flūr-dē-lē)´* - This is the jeweler's mark for the city of Verdun, France. The term means "flower of light". The *fleur-de-lis* is the French symbol of life and power, and is designed from nature's Iris. This symbol is found on many Victorian, Edwardian, and *Art Nouveau*, pieces and has been carried out in modern designs as well.

Fobs - The terms "fobs" and "charms" were interchangeable from mid 1850 through the 1930's.
Watch fobs or watch charms were in vogue in the 1890's through the turn-of-the-century and certainly on into the '30's when the pocket watch became more popular than ever. They were very desirable in agate, hematite, tiger eye, lava stone, convex crystal, goldstone, inlaid onyx or assorted onyx. (Plates 24-25-37)

Frame (see Mountings)

French Electric Jewelry - In 1875, master jewelers in France fashioned a unique and finely wrought piece of jewelry. The design cleverly concealed a thin wire in vest pocket (men) or hidden down the back of the dress or under hairdo (women). Electric impulses from a battery animated the object, such as moving the eyes, opening the mouth, fluttering the wings, etc. A truly novel conceit utilized in a stickpin for an ascot, or ornament for an *aigrette*.

"French Ivory" (also see Celluloid) - An imitation of ivory tusk in gained Celluloid or plastic. "French Ivory" is a registered trademark. Other ivory imitations, not quite as good, were *Ivorette, Ivorine, Ivory Pyralin,* and *DuBarry Pyralin.* In the 1870's, there was a shortage of ivory for billiard balls and a $10,000 prize was offered for anyone who could produce a substitute. John Wesley Hyatt mixed nitric acid and cellulose to make Celluloid. It was the first plastic to look like ivory. "French Ivory" products were produced by J. B. Ash Co. of Rockford, Illinois. Since Celluloid was highly flammable, it was eventually replaced by the use of Bakelite and other fire-retardant plastics.

French Jet - This is imitation black glass. The name "French" is a misnomer since most of the so-called "French jet" is actually from Bohemia (Czech.). It is a term which takes in almost all black sets, other than that which is genuine, such as jet and onyx.

Gems/Gemstones - Genuine gems and gemstones are created by natural mysterious forces.

Traditionally, the precious gems are: diamond, ruby, sapphire, and emerald. All other stones were considered "semi-precious". The modern view is that other gems are "precious" according to one's individual taste or preference. Therefore, the preferable terms for classifying all natural stones are: *precious gems* (diamond, ruby, sapphire, and emerald); *gemstones*: all other natural stones.

The faceted portion of a gem or gemstone (the top of the stone) is called the "table"; the bottom of the stone is called the "pavillion"; the point or the center is known as the "culet."

For many centuries past, jewels were considered medicinal. It was believed that some stones possessed unquestioned healing power. Hebrew tradition states that the Tablets of Moses were of sapphire, and the Hebrew word "sappir" means "the most beautiful". It symbolizes loyalty, justice, beauty, and nobility.

Emeralds from India, Persia, and Peru are the most valuable, and are shown as the emblem of charity, hope, joy and abundance. It also has the reputation of curing epilepsy and being an all-around pain-killer. St. John writes of the emerald in his Apocalypse.

The diamond has always been regarded as the most precious stone. It was believed that if a guilty person wore a diamond, it turned red; but in the presence of innocence it would retain its original purity and brilliance. The diamond was reputed to be a preserver against epidemics and poisons, that it calmed anger and formented conjugal love. The ancients called it "the stone of reconciliation". It symbolizes constancy, strength, and innocence.

In ancient times, the opal was considered a splendid stone but due to the belief that it attracted misfortune, it had the effect of lowering the desirability of the stone except for those who were born in October. This, of course, was a mere superstition which seemed to have been founded on a Russian legend which had come into France. It was reported that the Empress Eugenie had a horror of the opal and at the sight of one in the *Tuilleries*, she was actually terrorized.

The language of gems, their significance, and the superstitions connected with gems and gemstones have been documented in great depth in many books on stones and lapidary work. In fact, whole volumes have been written about the curiosity of gems, gems as talismans, and so forth. It is another fascinating aspect of jewelry, which deserves pursuit.

It is always fashionable, among lovers and friends, to note the significance attached to various gems and gemstones, and to give these for birthdays, engagement, and wedding presents:

Birthstones And Their Significance

MONTH	STONE	
JANUARY	Garnet	Insures constancy, true friendship and fidelity.
FEBRUARY	Amethyst or Pearl	Freedom from passion and from care.
MARCH	Bloodstone or Hyacinth	Courage,wisdom, and firmness in affection.
APRIL	Diamond	Emblem of innocence and purity.
MAY	Emerald	Discovers false friends and insures true love
JUNE	Agate or Cat's Eye	Insures long life, health and prosperity.
JULY	Coral or Ruby	Discovers poison, corrects evils resulting from mistaken friendship.
AUGUST	Sardonyx or Moonstone	Without it, no conjugal felicity, so must live unloved and alone.
SEPTEMBER	Chrysolite or Sapphire	Frees from evil passions and sadness of the mind.
OCTOBER	Opal	Denotes hope and sharpens the sight and faith of the possessor.
NOVEMBER	Topaz	Fidelity and friendship. Prevents bad dreams.
DECEMBER	Turquoise or Lapis Lazuli	Success and prosperity in love.

German Silver - Metal which has no actual silver content but is an alloy of copper, zinc, and nickel, with the highest content of nickel giving it a silvery-white color. It is a common base for plating. Also called "nickel silver", "French grey", or "gun metal".

Gilt (or Gilded) - A process for plating a die-stamped or hand-wrought piece of base metal to give it a gold color (see *Vermeil*). The gilding is inferior to rolled plate or electroplating.

"Glasgow Four" - C. R. Mackintosh, Herbert McNair and the sisters, Margaret and Frances MacDonald, to whom they were wed. Although Mackintosh and McNair worked in the Celtic style, rather than in the "high" *Art Nouveau* of the French, their designs greatly influenced the "modern movement" in Austria, Belgium, and Germany. However, when it came to jewelry, it was their wives who were most productive and influential to both their husbands' work and the art of "modern" jewelry. Their work was vital right through the Art Deco period.

Gold (also see Carat) - Precious metal ore containing alloys which vary depending on desired color and hardness.

Gold colors range from green to dull yellow, to bright pink and even red. White color, (color of platinum or silver), is achieved by alloying nickel and a small percentage of platinum to gold; thus, "White Gold" is an alloy of gold with silver, palladium, platinum, or nickel.

Platinum is more a 20th Century metal and is rarely represented in Victorian jewelry.

Gold is twice as heavy as silver, which is perhaps the reason why a more solid silver was used while gold was plated, filled, or rolled with inferior alloys. Platinum is even heavier than gold which explains why it is seldom used for *baroque* pieces.

The term "carat" or "karat" is for the fineness of gold. Example: 18K or 750 = 18/24 or 750/1000th which represents 75% pure gold content.

Gold-Filled - Joining a layer or layers of gold alloy to a base metal alloy, then rolling or drawing as required for thickness of material.

Goldstone - Adventurine gemstone sparkling with particles of gold-colored minerals; or, man-made brown glass with specks of copper infused within.

Granular Work - Gold or silver metal applied in decorative designs which resemble tiny grains or pin-heads, roundly shaped.

Gypsy Setting (also known as Bezel) - Where top of stone is exposed just above the metal casing.

Hair Ornaments (also see Combs) - Hair ornaments were worn from 1850 through the 1925 era. They were executed in both gold and sterling silver. Most of the metal was cut, pierced, or engraved, with some fine *repousse'* work. Later there were synthetics such as Celluloid.

Hair ornaments ordinarily have a pair of teeth whereas combs, which often were made in the same styling, had as many as four to nine teeth, depending on the size of the comb. (Plates 2-45)

Hair Pins - The Tortoise Brand trade-mark was that of Rice & Hochster Makers, New York, and sold for 25ᶜ per dozen boxes. They were made in three shapes: straight, loop, and crimped; being available in three colors: shell, amber, and black.

The "Gibson Girl" hairdo at the height of its popularity, required many hair pins in order to keep the *coiffure* neat and in place. This hair style required a great deal of not only one's natural hair but additional tresses to give it fullness and beauty. To keep the extra hair pieces, hair switches, and wigs in place, it was necessary to use many hair pins plus two or three combs. (Plate 2)

Hair pins were made of rolled gold decorated with birds, butterflies, and stars and these were worn in great profusion throughout the headdress.

In 1921, Swartchild & Co., Chicago, advertised in their catalogue: "The Neverslip Hairpin" for holding eyeglass-chain securely in the hair. The chain extended from the end curve of the hair pin to the small loop at the side of the spectacles or eye glasses.

Hallmark - An official mark first adopted in England which is incised, punched, or stamped on gold or silver to show quality and to signify purity of metal according to "sterling" or "carat" standard. Other countries' hallmarks indicate origin, patent, manufacture, etc. Most of the countries in Europe stamped their gold and silver wares with "hallmarks". As early as 1363, England had already passed laws saying that every master goldsmith shall have a "quote by himself", and the same mark "shall be known by them which shall be assigned by the King to survey their work allay". That meant that all the goldsmiths' work had to be assayed before they could be put on the mark which was ordained by the King. Such marks would certify the ore content of both the silver and the gold.

By 1857, the word "Sterling" became universally used except in the United States. Until 1894, no State protection was given to purchases of either gold or silver, and the buyer could only trust the reputation of the maker and dealer.

State laws regulating the stamping of the words "Sterling", "Sterling Silver", "Coin," or "Coin Silver" on wares of silver or metals purporting to be silver, were first passed in 1894, Massachusetts being the leader in this regard; but many other States followed suit within the next ten years. These laws were similar within each State and they specified that any wares which were marked "Sterling" or "Sterling Silver" must contain 925 parts of fine silver in every 1,000 parts. "Coin" or "Coin Silver", must contain 900 parts of fine silver in every 1,000. Persons were subject to misdemeanor charges if they attempted to sell merchandise that was marked "Sterling" or "Coin Silver" that did not contain the above-mentioned quantities of pure silver.

Regarding the hallmarking of gold, it had become law that no article was to be offered for sale that did not plainly stamp the exact number of twenty-fourth parts of pure gold or portion of gold that the said article contained. Any person found guilty of violation of the provisions of this act could be fined up to $1,000 or imprisoned in a "common jail" not to exceed one year, or both, "at the discretion of the court".

Hallmarking became so strict that even portions of a particular piece of jewelry had to be marked. For instance, the front of a pin could be marked "Sterling" and the back could be an alloy and it would have to be stamped thus: "Sterling front."

Trademarks should not be confused with hallmarks inasmuch as a trademark is the name of the manufacturing company of the artisan, whereas a hallmark is a guarantee of the quality of the ore contained in the merchandise.

Mass production brought new codes, and many European countries then allowed their retailers of jewelry to have their own mark; therefore, many manufacturers, craftsmen, designers, and/or artists, remain unknown. Liberty & Co., is a prime example: their artists were compelled to remain anonymous, and all "modern works" and "Orientalia" were marked or labelled with the Liberty trademark.

MARKS MISTAKEN FOR MANUFACTURER/DESIGNER/JEWELER
Rolled gold or silver plate or electro plate:

R.P. = rolled plate
E.P. = silver electro plate
G.F. = gold filled
N.S. = nickle silver
G.S. = German silver
B.M. = Britannia metal
W.M. = white metal

Hatpin - A hatpin was used to securely fasten a hat to the hair and head of the wearer. Hatpins measuring from 4" to 12" in length were worn from approximately 1850 to 1930.

It's interesting to note that in some of the early 1890 catalogues, there were two classifications for pins: 1) to secure a bonnet; 2) to secure a hat. Both were hatpins. It is difficult to distinguish one from the other except that the bonnet pin seems to be a bit smaller and the design of the ornament is more of the Victorian Age--somewhat *baroque*, perhaps with a starburst, a flower or a scabbard. The bonnet pins were made of gold plate or of a gold color such as the hair ornaments, whereas many hatpins were featured in sterling silver, and clearly were works of *Art Nouveau* artisans. (Plates 2-11-12-15-23-29-42-44-46)

Hatpins were a bit more daring than "bonnet" pins in that they had bowknots, insects, and designs inspired by shells and flowers. There was also a great deal of open work departing from the *baroque*-type of *repousse* which is so often found in hair ornaments and on the bonnet pins. Perhaps the advertisements for both bonnet pins and hatpins were to please some 1890's women who refrained from wearing the "masculine" hat, since most women still referred to head coverings as "bonnets". More traditional women preferred calling a hat a "bonnet", even when there were no longer ribbons tied under the chin but hung loosely at the sides. In that fashion, the strings were called "lappets".

By 1900, "bonnets" was no longer a term used in magazines published for women. The *Delineator* of 1900 thus reported: "Every woman of intelligence and good taste is aware that her hat either adds to or completely destroys the beauty of her toilette..."

Little *toques* and turbans were given every type of artifice to make them more attractive, such as plumes, quills, flowers, and rosettes of taffeta or chiffon; adding to the basic hat was a fashionable jet buckle or other type of hat ornament. Small *toques* and turbans were given every type of artifice to make them more attractive, such as plumes, quills, flowers, and rosettes of taffeta or chiffon; adding to the basic hat was a fashionable jet buckle or other type of hat ornament. Small *toques* were hats which set atop the Gibson Girl hairdo and were "speared and settled" by equally luxurious hatpins which often-times matched the buckles, hat and dress ornaments. To each millinery creation a note of brilliancy was added by rhinestone buckle, the jeweled ornament, and the several fashionable hatpins which had reached the height of popularity in 1900-1913.

In December 1910, there was an article in *The Five and Ten Cent Magazine* which stated that 1910 was "the greatest season for big hatpins in the history of the trade". Hatpins were large enough to hold powder puffs, mirrors, trinkets, and small change. They were being shown for the Christmas trade by the manufacturing jewelers. Guards were used to cover the dangerous points of the pins.

The author has written the first world-wide definitive work on the subject of hatpins titled, "The Collector's Encyclopedia of Hatpins and Hatpin Holders", published by Collector Books, Paducah, Kentucky. For those interested in pursuing the subject of hatpins in depth, the author suggests her aforementioned work first published in 1976.

Hematite *(hĕm′-a-tīt)* - A blood-like red iron ore which in the form of crystals is used primarily as settings for men's jewelry. Brown hematite, called limonite in modern-day usage, refers to either the reddish-brown or the brown color.

Illusion Setting - A setting in which the stone is made to appear larger by cutting metal in shape of gem-table.

Imitation (also see Synthetics) - To make out of other materials a substance resembling the natural element, i. e., paste or rhinestones for gems; hard rubber, dyed and then molded into coral-color flowers; plastic tortoise shell; "French Ivory", which is an imitation of ivory, bone, etc. *Imitation is not the same as synthetic.*

Intaglio *(in-tăl′-yo)* - To cut a design deeply on the obverse or front of a gem or other type material. *Intaglio* is the opposite of *repousse'*.

Iridescent - To give a high luster to glass, or other man-made materials.

Jade - A hard stone with a resinous or oily aspect when polished. Jade is not actually carved but is cut or chipped, chiseled, or ground into the desired size and shape, then polished. Jade is found in many shades, and the presence of quantities of iron determines the color. The colors vary: mutton fat (sometimes streaked with gray or brown tones); green (spinach or moss colors); celadon (off-white color); tangerine; pink; lavender; and the most desirable color, luminous apple-green called Imperial Jade.

Jade is formed into amulets, hair ornaments, rings, bracelets, beads, necklaces, pendants, and Chinese burial pieces called "weights" for the tongue and eyes.

Because jade is a tough, hard, resilient stone, it cannot be easily scratched, whereas imitation jade (called by many new names) can scratch. One of the most common imitations of jade is dyed calcite which is nothing more than ordinary marble, chalk or limestone.

Although jade occurs in Asia, America, and other countries, the Oriental jade is most desirable.

Nephrite jade, (white to dark green) is found on mainland China. Jadeite, (emerald to pale green, white, red-brown, yellow-brown, violet & pink) is from Burma.

Japanned - Japanning is a process of darkening iron wire by immersing in black japan, a by-product of coal.

Japonism (jăp´ ŏ-nĭz´m) - Japanese influence in the art of *cloisonne* enameling, lacquer work, and other Oriental wares, using plant motifs and curving lines which highly influenced the *Art Nouveau* artisans. Structure, expression, and quality of art, characteristic of the Japanese, i.e., two-dimensional graphics, etc.

Jewelers (1850-1935) - For biographical information about some note-worthy *Art Nouveau* and Art Deco jewelers, artisans, designers, manufacturers, and retailers of jewelry, refer to the section: Thumbnail Sketches and to the Bibliography that lists publications which offer more detailed accounts.

Jet (Genuine and Imitation) - Jet is the name given most black jewelry whether it be genuine or glass. Genuine jet will retain its sparkling polish for many years. "Black glass", (also known as "French Jet", even though most black glass came from Bohemia), will crack, scratch, and become dull.

Genuine jet is a brown-black lignite in which the texture or grain of the original fossilized wood of which this particular coal is comprised, can still be seen. It can be brought to a high polish and is thus easily imitated in glass. The finest genuine jet comes from Whitby (England), where over 200 workshops produced Victorian Era jewelry. Jet was associated purely with mourning, although it had been worn in earlier times as decorative jewelry. Jet jewelry was considered proper wear during the first year of mourning, then diamonds or pearls were allowable during the second period of mourning. During those first two years, a widow was expected to wear "widow's weeds" and at that time, no earrings were worn in the street. This was etiquette, circa 1850-1900. The Art Deco period, featured black and white geometric patterns that made black glass popular again.

"Jargow Nib" - A nickname used in 1913 for point protectors, named for Berlin's police-president von Jargold, who sought to enforce the wearing of hatpin "safeties" by law. First report of the "Jargow-nib" was in "New York Times", April 19, 1913.

Lapis Lazuli (lăp´-ĭs lăz´-ū-lī) - Deep blue gemstone, sometimes containing gold-colored specks of iron pyrites.

Lavaliere *(lăv´-á-lēr)* - Named for the Duchess de La Valliere, mistress of Louis XIV, (1644-1710), this type of jewelry is an ornament hanging from a chain which is worn around the neck. The terms *"lavaliere"* and *"pendant"* could be used interchangeably. However, *"lavaliere"* does not appear in jewelers' catalogues until after 1900.

Pendants and *lavalieres* both have small jump rings or fancy type loops into which a chain is threaded. Pendants, before the turn-of-the-century, had a heavy *baroque* type of drop, whereas those from 1900-1913 represent the more beautiful *lavalieres* of the *Art Nouveau* period. (Plates 14-19-35-44-47-49)

Limoges (enamel) *(le̅-mōzh´)* - A colorful application of enamel that depicts a portrait or scene similar to that which is rendered on canvas. (Plate 40)

Lockets - These ornaments hung from neck chains and bracelets, and were worn as charms or fobs. They were designed in ovals, rounds, hearts, and other varied shapes. Lockets opened to hold one, two, and often three or more photographs, as well as mementoes such as pressed flowers or a lock of hair. They were embossed, chased, engraved, enameled; many were set with gems and gemstones or had pictorial, floral, or *Art Nouveau* motifs in *repousse.*

Lockets were made of gold, silver, rolled gold and plate. The gold-front lockets for gentlemen, which were worn with their waist or vest chains, were larger and much more intricately worked and designed than other type lockets. The solid gold front of the locket called for high relief and design work and many were set with rubies and sapphires which accentuated a scenic engraving or portrait. The chased frames and edges of the lockets were finished with lovely chasing. The locket from 1890 through WWI was probably the most sentimental gift for men, women, and children. To this day, it still remains a highly prized piece of jewelry.

Lorgnette *(lôr´-nyĕt)* - A *lorgnette* is a pair of eye-glasses or an opera glass which is attached to a handle. A *lorgnon* is actually a single glass such as a monocle, but ordinarily speaking, *lorgnon* could be substituted for *lorgnette.*

Most *lorgnons* fold, and there were tiny ones that were made for *chatelaines*, and some that were so small, they were called "glove *lorgnons*".

Frames could be from simple to ornate. Some of these were jewel encrusted, or encased in tortoise-shell or mother-of-pearl and some had a crest engraved in gold. Shell and horn were best sellers and were made by European craftsmen.

There were wrist chains used especially for the glove *lorgnon*. Chains and *lorgnons* frequently go together and the same decorative treatment was usually applied to both. In 1880 *lorgnettes* made of zylonite (plastic) were offered for sale.

The *Art Nouveau* period produced exquisite *lorgnettes* that could fold in half on a small hinge and slide into the handle. The flowing *Art Nouveau* lines lent itself to this article and many of the *lorgnette* frames were jewel encrusted with curved handles that represented twisted stems of flowers or women with flowing hair.

Lorgnette chains were set with pearls, turquoise, rubies, opals, diamonds, imitation gems and gemstones. A swivel clasp was at the end of the chains to which spectacles, fans, or eye-glasses could be attached. Other type chains had a pin clasp for fastening to the clothing. The demise of the *lorgnette* came with the Great Depression of the 1930's when theaters and other places of luxury were less frequented; the sobering events dictated a less "affected" stance by high society in face of mass poverty.

Marcasite - A white iron pyrite. If the ore is yellow, it takes on the appearance of "fool's gold". Cut steel jewelry and marcasites resemble one another in color and in faceted treatment, but cut steel will rust easily and is not as hard nor as brilliant as marcasites. Most marcasite jewelry is made in France and is usually mounted in silver, although marcasites were also set into tortoise shell or plastic. Individually mounted marcasites are more desirable than machine-made casements or strips. (Plates 19-44-48)

Match Safe - This term, although an early expression, was familiar throughout the *Art Nouveau* period. The match safe was small compared to the larger version which came after 1905, when it was called "match boxes". They were made in either gold, silver, or plated base metals and were a favorite conceit for *Art Nouveau* motifs.

Matrix - An inferior or foreign substance that intrudes in or surrounds a gemstone such as Turquoise or Lapis Lazuli.

Mine Cut (or Old Mine Cut) - Gems from South America, mostly Brazil, before diamond mines were discovered in Africa. The cut differs from "European cut" in that it was thicker from the table of the gem to the bottom facet which was cut off flat.

Moonstone - Translucent gemstone with pearly or opaline luster.

Mother-of-Pearl - Differs from abalone in color in that it is the iridescent inner-shell layer of a pearl oyster.

Mosaic - Creating a motif or design in parquetry with tiny pieces of colored glass (or stone) which have been set into plaster. Individual portions of the design are sectioned by metal, similar to form used in *cloisonne* (*cloisons*). (Plate 14)

Mounting - The specific adaptation of a stone or artifact within a cage, frame, or setting, usually comprised of metal.

Necklaces (see Lavaliere)

Nibs - Small metal shafts used on the end of a pointed pin as a point-protector, shield or guard.

Niello (enameling) *(ni-ĕl-ō)* The lines or incisions of a design are con-trasted with the color of the metal, i.e., gold, silver, etc., by applying in several layers, a mixture of sulphur, lead, silver and copper which appears black when filled into the engraved metallic work. A blackish enamel work.

Nodder (also called "Bobbler", "Springer", "Trember", or "Tremblant") - A short spring which causes an ornamental head to bobble or bounce freely. Several short springs or wires could be utilized on a bouquet of metallic flowers set with brilliants which would then sparkle as they moved and caught the light.

Opalescence - A pearly sheen radiating from within a gem such as a moonstone.

Openwork (see Piercework)

Parure *(pȧ-roŏr)* - Matching jewelry containing several pieces such as necklace, choker, brooch, earrings, bracelet, and ring. *Demi-parure* con-sists of only two to three matching pieces.

Paste - A superior glass containing oxide of lead used for jewelry to imitate gems and gemstones. Joseph Strass perfected paste, although paste was used since ancient times as imitations of precious stones. Much paste is actually a composition of pounded rock crystal melted with alkaline salts, and colored with metallic oxides.

Some paste stones are set with bright foil, a thin leaf of metal placed in back of a gemstone or glass to heighten its brilliance. The finest quality paste, however, requires no foil or backing and it is usually claw-set or mounted as a genuine gem would be. Inferior paste may be backed with mercury or quicksilver and applied by machine rather than the more expen-sive handwork which requires each paste stone to be individually mounted.

The finest paste is hand-cut and faceted, treated like a "gem"; commercial pastes are molded. Unless one is an expert, superior paste is sometimes difficult to distinguish between diamonds, spinels, or other imitated gems.

Pate-de-Verre (Paste Glass) *(pä/tä-dĕ-vâr)* - Crystal and lead combined in a pulverized heavy paste compound which is then layered in a mold and kiln-fired. After cooling, the mold is broken; the result is a unique object rendered in muted hues of heavy glass. Designers and makers: Henry Berge,́ worked for *Daum Freres* c1897-1914; models for casting by A. Walter (1908), Joseph Cheret, J. B. Descomps, I. Cayette, Jules-Paul Brateua, Albert-Louis Dammouse. (Plate 12)

Pave ́ Setting *(pà-vā)́* - Stones placed so closely together that almost no metal shows between them.

Peacock-Eye Glass - A glass whose coloring resembles the "eye" of a peacock feather. (Plates 1-23-29)

Pearls (also see "Blister" Pearl) - Pearls are the natural formation of a secretion called "nacre". Nacre, an iridescent shell-like substance, coats the natural or man-induced irritant which forms a pearl. When the pearls are naturally formed they are called "Oriental". "Cultured" pearls are made by nature with the help of man. This man-induced process originated with and was patented by Kokichi Mikimoto, 1896.

Cultured and Oriental pearls both come from the oyster; however, there are fake pearls made with fish scales. Glass beads, covered by an iridescent wax-like coating are called "waxbead pearls". They originally came from Italy and Bohemia. The waxbead type will eventually turn a dullish beige color, whereas the Cultured or natural Oriental pearl will retain its high lusters.

Some pearls are formed in perfect rounds, others acquire a "blister" or *baroque* shape. Strings of perfectly matched round pearls are most valuable.

Fresh-water pearls are called "river pearls". Salt-water pearls are primarily mounted in 18-carat gold and platinum, while freshwater or river pearls are set in lower carat.

1915-1916 were the years that the odd-shaped iridescent pearl was in demand and most came from Italy's Murano Island where artificial pearls were nothing more than glass covered by a paste made of fish scales.

Pearls are thought of as being only off-white and iridescent in color, but they are found in variations of pink, grays, and the highly prized black pearl.

Peking Glass - When it is a light green glass, it is sometimes called "poor man's jade"; however, it is manufactured in many other shades of glass, imitating the myriad colors of jade. The original Peking glass is a product of China.

Pendants (also see Lavaliere) - In 1910 the vogue for low collars invited all sorts of pretty neck ornaments such as pendants, *lavalieres,* and brooches. The most favored was the pendant, which was often enhanced by a black *moire* ribbon rather than a chain.

The delicate metal work was invariably either gold or silver. Many of the beautiful *lavalieres* or pendants included applique, fine filigree, and wire work, and much of the metal had a very thin edge or depth. Enamel work was very popular and jewelry as a whole became much less *baroque* than in Victorian times.

Phoenix - A bird represented by the heron or eagle motif in Egyptian mythology. According to legend, it was consumed by fire but rose from its own ashes; thus, the Phoenix symbolizes ressurrection and an emblem of immortality. It also appears in Chinese symbolic motifs.

Pierce Work - Die-cast frame which is cut and engraved with a great deal of open work in the metal.

Pin - Origin of word thought to be from the Latin "spina", a thorn found on the Spina Christi tree. Natural thorns are still used as pinning devices in some parts of the world. A pin is a device for attaching or securing many things. It can be strictly functional, decorative, or both.

Pins (or Brooches) - Because yesteryear clothing lacked today's modern laundry conveniences, collars, cuffs, frills, ribbons, etc., were detachable. Many of the collars and cuffs, etc., were pinned in place by exquisite "lace pins" which were most often of delicate filigree or open work.

A small pin, which has long since been forgotten, was the novelty "safety pin" that came in around 1901. These were offered in 10-carat gold and were sometimes called "negligee collar pins". They resembled a very narrow barrett or bar pin. They were also called "handy pins", sold in pairs, in a myriad of design, executed in a gold front, gold filled, sterling silver, or black enamel.

The bar pin is usually a one to two inch horizontal of gold or silver, with many innovations and variations of the jeweler's art. It was worn at the collar or neckline of a woman's garment.

Sterling silver brooch pins were most often engraved or had open lacework or filigree work. The *baroque* scroll patterns were the most desirable in the earlier Victorian Era, but they gave way to *Art Nouveau* designs.

Cape or jersey pins were two pins attached by a chain. They were made in solid gold, rolled gold plate, and in sterling silver. Silver was the popular color metal for jewelry during the Arts and Crafts and *Art Nouveau* periods.

"Beauty pins" were in vogue during 1901-1910 period. They were worn in place of studs in the front of waists or blouses and came in threes or fours. They were very tiny, measuring no more than ¼" to ½" and were enameled with the most delicate flowers such as tiny violets or forget-me-nots. Most were beautifully enameled and in exquisite detail.

The main difference between pins and brooches is that pins are first utilitarian, and then decorative, whereas brooches are primarily decorative. Today we refer to all kinds of decorative brooches as pins or vice-versa.

Pique *(pē-kāʃ* - Inlaying of gold, silver, and mother-of-pearl overlay, or inlay of tortoise-shell, ivory, or horn.

Plastics (also see Bakelite and Celluloid) - Term applied to a group of synthetic chemical products with the distinctive quality which enables them to be molded, carved, laminated, or pressed into many shapes, sizes, and designs. Tortoise, horn, mother-of-pearl, wood, marble, jet, and amber were all imitated in plastics.

Some imitations for natural elements were called by other names, such as in case of tortoise: "tortone", advertised as "non-breakable" by E. & J. Bass, New York; "tortoisene", manufactured by Harry Maynard, Washington, D. C.

Wm. K. Potter established his genuine *Tortoise Shell Works* at Providence, R. I., and horn and Celluloid were produced by Alfred Burke & Co., Leominster, Mass., and Thomas Long Co. of Boston. Besides "French Ivory" being produced, there was also *"ivoire Parisienne"*, both products being imitation ivory.

As with fine French paste, plastic jewelry (particularly of the Art Deco period), is not really an imitation but an art form of itself.

Plique-́A-Jour *(plē-kā-̱ā-jèrʃ* - A translucent *cloisonne* in which there is no metal backing for the enamel work. During firing, a metal supportive base is used until firing ceases; then when the piece has cooled and the enamel has hardened, the finished product no longer requires the base, so this support is removed. (Plates 3-6-11-13-22-25-39-49)

Purses (Bags) - Most collectors may be surprised to learn that the frames of mesh bags were works of very fine jewelers. Diamonds and other precious stones were often threaded into the mesh, and the designs were actually executed in jewels. Some purses were made entirely of seed pearls. Enameling was extensive and lavish. Frames were rich with *repousse*, hand engraving or cutwork. Gemstones were introduced in the clasp or the chain. The bags were made as carefully as a jeweler would make a watch and many required no less than three months to complete because of the intricate workmanship.

Cut steel beads were very popular and bead bags, with conventional floral colors, were considered handsome and dressy. The frame usually matched the tone of the beads used.

Beaded purses were much less expensive than metallic mesh purses that demanded the very finest jeweler's art and ingenuity. Mesh bags were made with fancy weaves such as the star pattern, zig-zag, plaid, daisy pattern, basket weave, herring-bone, and even reversible mesh.

At the beginning of the 20th Century, the mesh purse went to the extreme, using pinks and greens, or purples and blue ostrich feathers dyed and then sewn right onto the purses. They were really much more daring and less conservative than the previous mesh and beaded bags that were square shaped. The *new* purses were of the triangular shape, so that coins would drop dead center into the "point" and not get lost.

"Opera and handkerchief bags" were in vogue during the autumn of 1910. They were reported to be delicately tinted suede embroidered in mock gems.

The frames, clasps, and chains were usually of gold and silver and were purchased separately. Many of the women's magazines had directions for making the various types of pouches which were then attached to the jeweled frames to complete the purse or bag. (Plates 33-36)

Unless marked "sterling," silver mesh purses were mainly of German silver or gun metal. Silver mesh purses were designed either with a drawstring, a bracelet loop, or with a finely detailed snap-type frame which was done with high relief work or set with imitation stones. Sterling mesh bags were manufactured by Weizenegger Bros., Newark, N. J., while Levitt & Gold, New York, made 14-karat and platinum mesh bags. Another famous American maker was Whiting-Davis, a company that made exquisite silver frames.

Beaded drawstring bags were highly fashionable accessories·in the "jazz age" of the "Roarin' Twenties." Many of these beaded drawstrings were imported from France and were of sterling, or gold frames set with precious stones.

Beaded bags always keep their beautiful, original color. Most beads are iridescent with high luster and are transparent. Silk thread being opaque, absorbed the color of the bead; the thread and the beads blend. In other words, purple beads were combined with a violet thread; light and medium blue beads with gray or other shades of blue thread, etc.

Bead makers described their wares as "...gold iridescent lusters and transparent iridescent beads. Radiant shades, such as golden brown, jade, green, violet, etc., are blended with tints of translucent gold in the same beads to make truly gorgeous bags..."

Repousseʹ *(rĕ-pōō-sā)ʹ* - Decorating metal by pushing out from behind or the reverse side in order to create a raised design in relief. The opposite of *intaglio.*

Rhinestone - At one time "rhinestones" meant rock crystals taken from the bed of the River Rhine, but this no longer applies. Thus, "rhinestone" takes its name but no element, from the River Rhine, Germany. It is a faceted glass stone, usually set with foil or painted backing to give it highlights. It is inferior to French paste or strass and once the backing is scratched or marred, it loses its luster.

Rim - The outside edge of a set stone.

Rings - The "father of jewelry" was Prometheus. According to Pliny, Hercules cut Prometheus loose from the chains which fastened the latter to Mount Caucasus. Prometheus supposedly made a ring out of one of the links, and bezel-set a portion of the rock against which he had been chained. This was considered the first ring and the first "gem".

There's a great deal of sweet romance and legend bound up in the wedding ring. When the first glow of Christianity lighted the world, Pliny the Elder told of a custom his people had borrowed from the ancients of the Nile, that of giving a ring of iron to pledge a betrothal. Such customs from the dim past and the ceremonies which thereby developed, have definitely changed from those early times.

In 1893, Prince Albert presented Queen Victoria with a wedding ring in the form of a serpent. Because of that presentation and the 1922 opening of King Tut's Tomb, the serpent motif is found in just about every form of jewelry from the early *Art Nouveau* & Art Deco Periods, into the late thirties.

In 1900, rings with colored stones were not in vogue for engagement rings. The fashionable engagement ring was a solitaire diamond or smaller stone set in a simple mounting.

"Anti-rheumatic" rings came in just before the turn-of-the-century. They were of gold shell on the outside with gray metal on the inside.

In 1901, *The Delineator* reported that beautiful rings "proper for a man", would be a solitaire diamond, a ruby, cat's eye, or other precious stone mounted in a gypsy or handsome carved gold setting.

Women did not consider rings their province until the early 18th Century. Prior to that, most men of nobility wore rings as seals. The period when rings were most commonly worn by both sexes was from 1875 to the present day.

"Token rings" were the most desirable gift for the betrothed from 1880 to around 1910. Such a ring, with clasped hands, was called "Mizpah". "Mizpah", translated, means: *"The Lord watch between me and thee when we are absent one from another".*

Rolled Gold - A thin leaf of gold used in plating lesser metals. Method varies from rolling to electroplating a coat of gold over an inferior metal.

Rose Cut - The faceting of a gem, genuine or imitation, before the turn-of-the-century. The brilliant-cut was not commonly used before 1905. But by 1920, the brilliant-cut faceting of diamonds and other gemstones was superior and did away with the ordinary rose-cut of the earlier era.

Roundels - Tiny round beads often used as separators.

Sautoir *(sō-twär)* - A term popularized in 1890 to designate a very long, narrow gold link chain with either a pearl, diamond, polished agate bead, etc., introduced at 1" or 2" intervals for the length of the chain. In most instances, the *sautoir* fell below the waistline and was held in place at the waist by a brooch. The chain was fastened together by a jeweled slide which prevented its separation at the bosom. Other *sautoirs* flaunted tassels which hung 3" to 6" longer, requiring the chain to be "tucked in" at the waistline.

In the first decade of the 20th Century, *sautoirs* were advertised in various jewelry catalogues as long chains with a center drop to accomodate detachable tassels, pendants, or other conceits. The term is now considered archaic, though it is sometimes revived as a term for the extremely long beaded necklaces of the twenties.

Some *sautoirs* are termed: 20" chains with center drop chains measuring 6" to 8" from which ornaments can be hung; also, as long strings of chains or beads or pearls ending with 2" to 4" tassels.

Scarabus (Scarab) - Form of a beetle, the Egyptian symbol of longevity. (Plate 1)

Scarf Pins (also see Stickpins and Tie Pins) - Scarf pins were made for both ladies and gentlemen as seen in the 1890-1930 catalogues. By the 1920's, they were already being called "cravat" and "tie pins" for men, and "scarf pins" for women.

No distinction was made between male or female styles. Many of the pins had a spiral device which kept them from slipping out; others had fancy innovations such as small shafts at the heads which would secure them against slippage or loss.

Scarf pins offered no end to diversity of design and were set with gems, gemstones, imitation stones, and synthetics.

Advertisements for scarf pins most often read: "set with brilliants" which usually referred to a glass "diamond" or doublet of a popular gem such as garnet, opal, ruby, moonstone, or turquoise.

Secession (or Sezezzion) - An "anti-historical" style of *Art Nouveau* jewelry from Austria and Czechoslovakia, strongest movement in Vienna. (*Sezessionist* abstracts were the basis for much Scandinavian "*nouveau*" jewelry.)

Setting (see specific type) - A means of incorporating gems, gemstones (genuine, synthetic, or imitation), into metal or other elements, with designs known as: Bezel, Box, Channel, Claw, Gypsy, Crown, Illusion, Metal Cup (rhinestones), *Pave* and Tiffany.

Shank - A circle forming a ring, or that portion of a ring which is finally joined to the center mounting or focal point. A pin-shank is the utilitarian portion of a brooch, stickpin, or hatpin, which is attached to the ornamental object.

Silver-Deposit Ware - Glass decorated with silver overlay.

Silver Gilt (see Vermeil) - Silver with a thin coat of gold or yellow lacquer to produce a rich golden color.

Slides - French slides were mass-produced in gold-filled or gilded-metal. The design depended on raised work and enamels rather than jewels.

English slides relied heavily on inlay work incorporating large pieces of bloodstone, carnelian, and onyx, set into 9 to 18 carat. Others of less artistry were of rolled gold and silver.

American slides braved the brilliance of many gemstones set into delicately engraved, tiny slides. Larger slides housed garnets, onyx, cameos, rubies, diamonds, and emeralds, with much Etruscan-style intricacy or granular work.

Slides are to be found in round, flat, square, oblong, oval, barrel-shaped and other metallic improvisations executed in low carat to 18 carat, gold filled, rolled gold and silver. They range in size from ¼" to 2", with tubular findings to permit passage of a chain. Other slides allowed chains to pass through two holes on either side of slide which was cork-filled to prevent slippage. (Plate 28)

Slides have become collectible for handsome bracelets. Be alert to the fine *copies* of slides which are in the marketplace.

Springers (see Nodder)

Square-Cut Stone - Another cut for gems, which is in a square.

Sterling - A British term referring to the highest standard of silver which has a fixed standard of purity: 925 parts of silver to 75 parts copper.

The word originated with immigrant Germans who came across the Channel to England. They settled in a geographic area from which they took the name "Easterlings". Jewelers by trade, they were called upon to refine silver for coinage, and in 1343 the first two letters were dropped from

162

the word "Easterling", resulting in the nomenclature--"sterling". It denotes the highest purity of silver. All British sterling is hallmarked.

Sterling silver, besides being utilized for conventional and familiar pieces of jewelry, was also produced as: veil clasps, ornamentation for elastic garters, ornately executed sash slides and buckles, additional trimmings for silk and grosgrain belts, hat marks, folding pocket combs, key rings, umbrella straps, bag or trunk checks, belt buckles, slides, ladies hat-band buckles, armlets (garters), and frames for purses and bags--all with *Nouveau* motifs in silver, the preferred metal for this design period in Great Britain, Germany, Bohemia, and Scandinavia.

Stickpin (Tie Pin, Scarf Pin, Ascot Pin) - Edwardians made frequent use of jewels in men's neckwear because of the popularity of the wide tie which could be beautifully accented by stickpins.

From approximately 1870 into the 20th Century, men and women of carriage wore stickpins in their hunting stock, scarves, or cravats; many were stylized forms of the riding crop, the fox, horse's head, or a hunting dog. It was in the Edwardian Era ("high" *Art Nouveau*), that the jeweler's imagination soared, providing today's collector with innumerable miniature works of art conceived in the ornament atop the stickpin.

Many prize stickpins have been converted into charms or brooches.

Stickpins were set with pearls, turquoise, diamonds, opals, rubies, amethysts, moonstone, coral, and even bezel-set hard-back beetles. There were also their counterpart in glass or paste.

Strass (Stras or Strasser) - Brilliant lead glass perfected by Josef Strass, for whom it was named. It is used in creating fine jewelry with artificial gems or gemstones, sometimes known as "French Paste".

Swivel (or Tongue Clip) - A prong-snap connector which is mounted in a movable part, then joined by a hook-ring which is connected to the ends of watch chains into which the watch is snapped and hung. Also utilized on *chatelaines*. (Plate 28)

Swizzlestick - A vanity conceit carried by both men and women before the turn-of-the-century, but more often by the former. It was in demand with the introduction of sea-going passenger ships.

The swizzel stick extended into an umbrella of fine wires which were then swirled in a glass of champagne to reduce the carbonation. In reducing the carbonating bubbles, champagne becomes a white wine which is more easily digestible thus reducing the cause of sea-sickness.

It was considered a gentlemanly practice to take a swizzle stick, (often worn on a long chain and stored in the pocket), and use the extended swizzle by swishing it in the beverage before offering it to a lady.

It not only prevented sea-sickness, but avoided "spotting" powder or rouge. In yesteryear, only heavy loose powder was available, unlike the solid-cake manufactured today. In addition, swizzle sticks (by reducing carbonation), lessened the chances of a lady belching in "polite society".

Swizzle sticks are still being manufactured by Tiffany & Co., but are worn more as a fad or fancy.

Synthetic - The term differs from "imitation" or "artificial." Synthetic stones are created by man's intelligent application of the chemicals which nature has produced through natural means. When referring to synthetic gems or gemstones, look to the recent developments of man-made diamonds from pure carbon and the Chatham emeralds which are a synthetic speeding-up process of obtaining emeralds.

In the art of synthesizing, man attempts to duplicate nature, whereas in chemical imitations, man seeks to merely imitate nature, and in glass there are the artificial gems.

Doublets and triplets are stones consisting of two or more layers of artificial materials which are adhered to the top layer of a genuine stone. If one were to remove a doublet, triplet, or quadruplet from its setting and look at it from the side, the materials can be seen where they were glued together. Ordinarily, a fine paste or a glass substance is glued to the genuine stone which makes the gem appear larger. This process is not considered either synthetic or imitation.

A fine example of man's ingenuity for creating a synthetic product is the cultured pearl, which is produced by man creating an "unnatural" irritation within the oyster's shell. Technically, a cultured pearl could be called synthetic, but since it is not "manufactured" by man but is rather produced by the workings of nature, it is called "cultured."

With man harnessing the atom, and with more understanding of the workings of the configuration of atoms, it is not too far reaching to suppose that some day all gems will be synthetically as well as naturally produced.

Tiara - The word is derived from a royal Persian headdress but is now accepted as any decorative jeweled or flowered headband or semi-circle worn by women for formal wear. The difference between a tiara and a diadem is that the latter is worn as a symbol of power or a crown of dignity.

Tie Pin (see Stickpin) - The term is synonymous with stickpin. The tie clasps or holders, (a term used interchangeably), were in all metals, many with raised polished edges, gray and Roman finish, satin finish, rose and other gold finishes. They were engraved, had bright bevelled edges, and were finished in colored enamels. (Plates 28-47)

Topaz - A gemstone with the characteristic color of yellow which varies from canary to deep orange. In natural form it consists of translucent or opaque masses, or transparent prismatic crystals found in white, greenish or bluish colors. When some specimens are heated, they become pink or red. A yellow variety of quartz, namely citrine, is sometimes called "false topaz".

Tortoise-Shell - Yellowish-brown grained substance which is the hardplate shell from the back of the tortoise. Imitation tortoise shell was manufactured from plastic. Sadler Bros., South Attleboro, Mass., made imitation *Tortoisene*. Tortoise was used primarily for combs and hair ornaments, as well as fine examples of the *Nouveau* jewelry (Also see *Pique*) (Plate 15)

Trade-Marks (see Hallmarks)

Trembler (or Tremblant) - A spring or wire mounted to an ornament to cause motion. The action gives a "nodder" effect. When used in conjunction with stones set into a floral pattern, mounted on coil or straight-wire springs, it creates a fascinating dance of light which is reflected from the moving gems.

Triangular Cut - A cut for gemstones, in a triangular shape.

Vermicelli *(vûr-mĭ-sĕl-ĭ)* - Italian for "little worms", used to describe thin gold wire twisted in a decorative design which "squirms like tiny worms". *Vermicelli* is not to be confused with granular work.

Vermeil *(vûr mĭl)* - Silver, bronze, or copper that has been gilded. Also a red (vermillion color) varnish applied to gilded surface to give high luster.

Victorian Era (1837-1901) - The 64-year reign of Queen Victoria, during which there were vast political and social changes, a rapid growth of industrialization, but a retention of strict moral rules and decorum which were challenged during the last half of her reign. "Victorian" now implies a "straight-laced, old fashioned" approach to both morals and standards. The Victorian Era was, in fact, a time of great change from the Dark Ages to an Age of Enlightenment.

Vinaigrette *(vĭn-ā-ā-grĕt)* - A small conceit usually executed in gold or silver, with perforations on the top for holding aromatic vinegar, smelling salts, etc.

Watches and Wrist Watches - Manufacturers of watches before the turn-of-the-century are written about in many fine volumes. Some of the more interesting places to find and identify a watch in your own possession would be in the catalogues of the period. There you will find not only replicas but exact descriptions, right down to the jewels in the setting, the type balance, the hair-spring, and the compensation-balance.

Ladies' watches were smaller replicas of men's watches and were worn on a *chatelaine* or a watch pin.

Up until WWI, the pocket watch and the decorative lapel watch were fashionable, but with the wearing of military uniforms and with women attending factory work in clothing untypical of that worn in the past, both sexes adopted the wrist watch, first initiated in the British army.

From 1910-1920, ladies' wrist watches were called bracelet watches and were convertible as either a pin or a bracelet. Wrist watches first introduced for women had a wrist band of fine crochet thread.

From 1920-1930, there were very stylish Art Deco evening watches for men, worn without a chain. They were merely slipped into the vest pocket. Some of the flat watches for men held a combination cigar cutter.

Zircon - A transparent gem that is found in yellow, brown, red, pink, etc., and is often used in birthstone rings as alternates for precious gems.

Zircon-Cut - Similar to faceted rose-cut diamonds.

SECTION V

CHAPTER I
CROSS-REFERENCE INDEX

CHAPTER II
ABOUT PRICING

CHAPTER III
VALUE GUIDE

CHAPTER I
CROSS-REFERENCE INDEX

CHAPTER II
ABOUT PRICING

The world's leading firm of art auctioneers, Sotheby Parke Bernet, held auctions of *Art Nouveau* jewelry over a nine month period during 1979-80. It was their considered opinion that prices for certain pieces would bring from $500-$5,000. The jewelry realized $3,200. - $27,000., respectively!

This is somewhat startling but substantial evidence that there are buyers and collectors of *Nouveau* jewelry who will bid against each other for the privilege of owning pieces of this unique period that produced such decorative and "decandent" examples of the jeweler's art, imagination, and creativity.

Art Deco jewelry is also being sought by avid collectors, and one can assume that market prices and auction prices will follow the lead set by *Art Nouveau* sales.

There's still a "shopper's market" for good quality and beautiful representative "new art" period jewelry at antique shops and shows. However, interest in *nouveau* and deco jewelry has been heightened by the steady flow of articles and publications about this formidable period representing such radical changes in every facet of human endeavor. This is particularly evident in the field of personal adornment.

Art Nouveau and Art Deco jewelry of perhaps less intrinsic value, has become collectible for its artistic merit, and therefore many jewelry pieces bring high prices for unique design rather than for actual worth of gems or value of the precious metals.

NOTE: The current values in this book should be used only as a guide. They are not intended to set prices, which vary from one section of the country to the another. Auction prices as well as dealer prices vary greatly and are affected by condition as well as demand. Neither the Author nor the Publisher assumes responsibility for any losses that might be incurred as a result of consulting this guide. Values are for individual pieces as shown on each plate, and relate to these *exact pieces*, as described, in each specific collection.

CHAPTER III
VALUE GUIDE

Plate 1
Top, belt buckle $75.00
Center, decorative buckle $85.00
Bottom, brooch $60.00
Plate 2
Row 1, brooch $20.00
Row 2, brooch $35.00
Row 3, left, brooch $8.00
   right, brooch $45.00
Row 4, left to right, hatpin $65.00
   hatpin $110.00
   necklace $125.00
   pr. hair pins   pr. $12.00
Plate 3
Row 1, brooch $850.00
Row 2, pendant $2,000.00
Row 3, left, brooch $350.00
Row 3, right, pin w/watch
   hook $375.00
Row 4, brooch $400.00
Row 5, pendant w/chain $2,500.00
Plate 4
Top, brooch $85.00
Middle, brooch $125.00
Bottom, brooch $75.00
Plate 5
Top, three necklaces ea. $40.00
Center, earrings $25.00
Bottom, necklace $35.00
Plate 6
Left to right, pendant $785.00
   pendant w/chain $1,250.00
   pendant w/chain $585.00
Plate 7
Top, left to right, ring $435.00
   ring $365.00
   ring $385.00
Bottom, left to right, ring $385.00
   ring $365.00
   ring $385.00
Plate 8
Top, belt buckle $15.00
Center, purse frame $110.00
Bottom, trio of lady's stud bottoms   set
   $60.00
Plate 9
Left to right, necklace $95.00
   necklace $75.00
   necklace $85.00

Plate 10
Row 1, left to right, brooch $200.00
   pendant w/chain $375.00
   brooch $275.00
Row 2, left to right, brooch $325.00
   brooch $325.00
   locket $225.00
Row 3, left to right, brooch $175.00
   brooch $525.00
   watch holder $150.00
Row 4, left to right, brooch $175.00
   brooch $325.00
   brooch $225.00
Plate 11
Row 1, left, pendant w/chain $785.00
   pendant w/chain $585.00
   right, bracelet $650.00
Row 2, left, pendant $950.00 center,
   pendant $1,000.00
Bottom, left, three
   hatpins $250.00-$350.00 +
Center, brooch $450.00
Lower right, pendant $385.00
Plate 12
Hatpin $175.00
Pendant $450.00
Plate 13
Left to right, pendant w/chain $485.00
   pendant without
   chain $895.00
   pendant w/chain $785.00
Plate 14
Row 1, brooch $25.00
Row 2, brooch $75.00
Row 3, *lavaliere* $250.00
Row 4, 2/pc. buckle $85.00
Plate 15
Left, hatpin $65.00
Top right, pr. pompadour combs   pr.
   $75.00
Bottom right, back comb $125.00
Plate 16
Earrings $425.00
Plate 17
Left, ring $385.00
Right, pendant w/chain $485.00
Plate 18
Top, brooch $20.00
Center, brooch $15.00

Bottom, brooch $45.00
Plate 19
Row 1, center top, pendant
    w/chain $95.00
Center (middle) necklace $135.00
Center (bottom) necklace $185.00
Row 2, left to right, dress clip $65.00
    pendant $85.00
    brooch $55.00
Row 3, bracelet $145.00
Row 4, bracelet $185.00
Row 5, left to right, earrings
    w/posts $125.00
    lavaliere $115.00
    earrings w/clips $125.00
Plate 20
Row 1, pendant w/chain $235.00
Row 2, 2/pc. buckle $245.00
Row 3, brooch $45.00
Row 4, left to right, hatpin $65.00
    hatpin . $75.00
    hatpin $65.00
Plate 21
Top, bracelet $25.00
Center, bracelet $35.00
Bottom, clip earrings $30.00
Plate 22
Pendant w/chain $1,250.00
Plate 23
Row 1, buckle w/safety pin $35.00
Row 2, left, scarf holder
    (sliding) $35.00
    right, cross $25.00
Row 3, set of 3 pins   set $35.00
Row 4, 2/pc buckle $75.00
    hatpin $85.00
Plate 24
Row 1, left to right, watch
    chain $65.00
    watch chain $325.00
    brooch $275.00
Row 2, left to right, brooch $325.00
    brooch $375.00
    brooch $450.00
Row 3, left to right, brooch $425.00
    pendant $100.00
    watch fob $175.00
Row 4, center, brooch $425.00
Row 5, center, belt buckle $425.00
    right, brooch $275.00
Plate 25
Row 1, center, pendant $685.00
Row 2, left, pendant w/chain $685.00

center, pendant
    w/chain $1,200.00
right, pendant
    w/chain $785.00
Row 3, left, pendant $685.00
    center, pendant $585.00
    right, watch fob $850.00
Row 4, left, pendant $245.00
    center, pendant
    w/chain $485.00
    right, pendant $585.00
Row 5, left, pendant w/chain $785.00
    center, pendant
    w/chain $685.00
    right, pendant
    w/chain $1,000.00
Plate 26
Left to right, pendant $585.00
    brooch $485.00
    pendant $485.00
Plate 27
Brooch or scarf pin $285.00
Plate 28
Top, Row 1, necklace $450.00
Row 2, left, woman's watch $650.00
    center, slides-bracelet $1,850.00
    right, watch $1,750.00
Row 3, left, knife w/pencil $285.00
Row 3, center, money clip $385.00
    (price guide does not include
    value of gold coin)
    right, tie clip $185.00
Row 4, bottom, watch chain
    w/slide $250.00
Plate 29
Row 1, brooch $55.00
Row 2, left, buckle $35.00
    right, hatpin $55.00
Row 3, left, brooch $75.00
    right, buckle $15.00
Row 4, hatpin $45.00
Plate 30
Top to bottom, bar pin $1,500.00
    brooch $95.00
    necklace $850.00
    brooch $185.00
    pendant $95.00
Plate 31
Top, ornamental comb $75.00
Center, brooch $35.00
Bottom, side comb $65.00
Left, necklace $35.00
Right, necklace $45.00

Plate 32
Left to right, pendant w/chain $385.00
    brooch w/hinged pendant
    loop $235.00
    pendant w/chain $485.00
Plate 33
Top, *chatelaine* hook
    w/purse $850.00
Row 2, left, brooch $185.00
    right, locket $400.00
Center, brooch on mesh
    purse $300.00
Bottom, necklace $2,800.00
Plate 34
Row 1, left to right, pendant $55.00
    pendant w/chain $250.00
    pendant $125.00
Row 2, bracelet $225.00
Row 3, necklace $150.00
Row 4, two brooches each $65.00
Row 5, necklace $225.00
Plate 35
Left to right, pendant w/chain $685.00
    lavaliere $385.00
    pendant w/chain $685.00
Plate 36
Top, coin purse $55.00
Center, purse $110.00
    buckle $95.00
Plate 37
Top, brooch $125.00
Row 2, left to right, brooch $225.00
    brooch $165.00
    watch fob $275.00
Row 3, left, brooch $300.00
    right, brooch $450.00
Row 4, left to right, brooch $225.00
    brooch $375.00
    brooch $175.00
Plate 38
Stickpin $185.00
Plate 39
Brooch $15,000.00
Plate 40
Assorted buttons $2.00 to $125.00
Plate 41
Cameo pendant w/chain $250.00
Plate 42
Row 1, Top, hatpin $45.00
Row 2, 2/pc buckle $20.00
Row 3, bracelet $85.00
Row 4, brooch $35.00

Plate 43
Row 1, left to right, pendant
    w/chain $250.00
    brooch $125.00
    pendant w/chain $250.00
Row 2, left to right, brooch $125.00
    pendant $200.00
    brooch $250.00
Row 3, left to right, pendant $300.00
    pendant $250.00
    pendant $350.00
Plate 44
Row 1, left to right, hatpin $250.00
    hatpin $65.00
    lavaliere $350.00
Row 2, left to right, rings: $385.00;
    $585.00; $385.00
Row 3, left to right, rings: $95.00;
    $145.00; $110.00; $110.00
Row 4, left to right, rings: $585.00;
    $1,000.00; $785.00
Row 5, bracelet $1,000.00
Row 6, pendant w/chain $1,750.00
Row 7, bracelet $45.00
Plate 45
Row 1, pendant w/chain $600.00
Row 2, left, brooch $95.00
    right, brooch $95.00
Row 3, brooch $350.00
Row 4, brooch $150.00
Row 5, left, ornamental hair
    comb $85.00
    right, decorative hair
    pin $135.00
Plate 46
Top, button $45.00
Center, hatpin $85.00
    pin $35.00
Bottom, necklace $350.00
Plate 47
Row 1, left, brooch $125.00
    right, pendant w/chain $100.00
Row 2, scarf pin $135.00
Row 3, *lavaliere* $275.00
Row 4, six stickpins $135.00 -
    $450.00
Plate 48
Row 1, 1/pc. buckle $35.00
Row 2, pr. shoe buckles $55.00
Row 3, left to right, 2/pc. belt
    buckle $35.00
    brooch $125.00
    2/pc. belt buckle $55.00

Row 4, pr. shoe buckles $65.00
Row 5, pr. shoe clips $35.00
Row 6, button $10.00
Plate 49
Row 1, left to right,
    pendant $1,250.00
    pendant w/chain $585.00
    pendant w/chain $425.00
    pendant w/chain $565.00
    pendant w/chain $750.00
Row 2, center, buckle $65.00
Row 3, left to right, pendant $485.00
    lavaliere $525.00
    pendant w/chain $585.00

Row 4, center, 2/pc. buckle $165.00
Row 5, center, brooch $45.00
Plate 50
Row 1, center, decorative sew-on
    buckle $65.00
Row 2, necklace $55.00
Row 3, left to right, 1/pc.
    buckle $85.00
    2/pc. buckle $225.00
    hatpin (head only) $55.00
Row 4, left to right,
    brooch $95.00
    brooch $185.00
    brooch $65.00

BIBLIOGRAPHY

ARTICLES

BAKER, STANLEY L., "Collecting Art Deco", *The Antique Trader*, Dubuque, Iowa. (Dec. 10, 1974)

BUCK, J. H. "Historical Sketch of Makers' Marks and Early American Legislation as to Silver", *The Jewelers' Circular Publishing Company*, New York. (1896)

GORDON, ELEANOR, and JEAN NERENBERG, "Early Plastic Jewelry", *The Antique Trader*, Dubuque, Iowa. (Nov. 26, 1974)

BOOKS

AMAYA, MARIO, *Art Nouveau*, E. P. Dutton and Co., Inc., New York. (1966)

ANSCOMBE, ISABELLE and CHARLOTTE GERE, *Arts and Crafts in Britain and America*, Rizzoli International Publications, Inc., New York. (1978)

BAINBRIDGE, HENRY CHARLES, *Peter Carl Faberge, Goldsmith and Jeweller to the Russian Imperial Court*, The Hamlyn Publishing Group, Ltd., London. (1966)

BAKER, LILLIAN, *The Collector's Encyclopedia of Hatpins and Hatpin Holders*, Collector Books, Paducah, Kentucky. (1976)

BAKER, LILLIAN, *One Hundred Years of Collectible Jewelry (1850-1950)*, Collector Books, Paducah, Kentucky. (1978)

BATTERSBY, MARTIN, *Art Nouveau, The Color Library of Art*, Paul Hamlyn. (1969)

BAUER, DR. JAROSLAV, *Minerals, Rocks and Precious Stones*, Octopus Books Limited, London. (1974)

BRADBURY, FREDERICK, F.S.A., *Bradbury's Book of Hallmarks*, J. W. Northend Ltd., West Street, Sheffield, S13SH, England. (1975)

BRADFORD, ERNLE, *Four Centuries of European Jewelry*, Spring Books, Hamlyn House, The Centre, Feltham, Middlesex. (1967)

DARLING, ADA W., *The Jeweled Trail*, Wallace-Holmstead Book Company, Des Moines, Iowa. (1971)

FALKINER, RICHARD, *Investing in Antique Jewelry*, Clarkson N. Potter, Inc., New York. (1968)

FLOWER, MARGARET, *Victorian Jewellery*, A. S. Barnes and Co., Inc., Cranbury, New Jersey 08512. (1967)

173

FRANK, JOAN, *The Beauty of Jewelry*, Crescent Colour Library International, Ltd. (1979)

FREGNAC, CLAUDE, *Jewelry from the Renaissance to Art Nouveau*, Octopus Books, Ltd., 59 Grosvenor St., London W1. (1973)

GARSIDE, ANNE, Editor, *Jewelry - Ancient to Modern (Walters Art Gallery)*, The Viking Press, 625 Madison Ave., New York NY 10022. (1980)

GERE, CHARLOTTE, *American and European Jewelry 1830-1914*, Crown Publishers, Inc., New York. (1975)

GILLON, EDMUND V., Jr., *Art Nouveau - An Anthology of Design and Illustration from the Studio*, Dover Publications, Inc., New York. (1969)

HASLAM, MALCOLM, *Marks and Monograms of the Modern Movement, 1875-1930*, Charles Scribner's Sons. (1977)

HILLIER, BEVIS, *Art Deco of the 20s and 30s*, Studio Vista/Dutton, New York. (1968)

HUGHES, GRAHAM, *The Art of Jewelry*, The Viking Press, Inc., 625 Madison Ave., New York, NY 10022. (1972)

HUGHES, GRAHAM, *Modern Jewelry*, Crown Publishers, Inc., 419 Park Ave. South,New York NY 10016. (1963)

JULIAN, PHILIPE, *The Triumph of Art Nouveau Paris Exhibition 1900*, Larousse &Co., Inc., 572 Fifth Ave., New York. (1974)

KOCH, ROBERT, *Louis C. Tiffany, Rebel in Glass*, Crown Publishers, Inc., NY. (1964)

LALIQUE, MARC ET MARIE-CLAUDE, *Lalique Par Lalique, copyright Societe Lalique*, Paris. (1977)

LEWIS, M. D. S., *Antique Paste Jewellry*, Boston Book and Art, Publishers, Boston, Massachusetts. (1970)

LESIEUTRE, ALAIN, *The Spirit and Splendor of Art Deco*, Paddington Press, Ltd., 30 E. 42nd St., New York. (1974)

MACKAY, JAMES, *Turn-of-the-Century Antiques*, E. P. Dutton Co., New York. (1974)

MADSEN, S. TSCHUDI, *Art Nouveau*, World University Library, McGraw-Hill. (Translated from Norwegian) (1967)

McCLINTON, KATHARINE MORRISON, *Lalique for Collectors*, Charles Scribner's Sons, New York. (1975)

MEBANE, JOHN, *The Complete Book of Collecting Art Nouveau*, Weathervane Books, New York. (1970)

MOUREY, GABRIEL, VALLANCE, AYMER, ET AL., *Art Nouveau Jewelry and Fans*, Dover Publishers Inc., New York. (1973)

MUCHA, ALPHONSE, MAURICE VERNEUIL AND GEORGES AURIOL, *Art Nouveau Design in Color*, Dover Publications, Inc. (1974)

NEWBLE, BRIAN, *Practical Enamelling and Jewelry Work*, The Viking Press, 625 Madison Ave., New York. (1967)

PERCY, CHRISTOPHER VANE, *The Glass of Lalique, (A Collector's Guide)*, Cassell & Colier Mac Millan Publishers, Ltd., 35 Red Lion Square, London, W CIR 4 SG. (1977)

READE, BRIAN, *Aubrey Beardsley*, Bonanza Books, a division of Crown Publishers, Inc., 419 Park Ave. South, New York, NY 10016. (1967)

RICKETTS, HOWARD, *Antique Gold and Enamelware in Color*, Doubleday & Co.

Inc., Garden City, New York. (1971)

ROSE, AUGUSTUS F. and ANTONIO CIRINO, *Jewelry Making and Design*, Dover Publications, Inc., New York. (1967)

RUTLAND, E. H., *An Introduction to the World's Gemstones*, Doubleday & Co. Inc., Garden City, New York. (1974)

SCHMUTZLER, ROBERT, *Art Nouveau*, Harry N. Abrams, Inc., 110 E. 59th St., New York, NY 10022. (1962)

SINKANKAS, JOHN. *Van Nostrand's Standard Catalog of Gems*, D. Van Nostrand Co., Inc., Princeton, New Jersey. (1968)

SJOBERG, JAN and OVE, *Working With Copper, Silver and Enamel*, Van Nostrand Reinhold Co., New York. (1974)

TAIT, HUGH and CHARLOTTE GERE, *The Jeweller's Art*, The British Museum. (1978)

URBAN, STANISLAV and ZUZANA PESTOVA, *Jablonec Costume Jewelry - An Historical Outline*, Museum of Glassware and Costume Jewelry, Jablonec, Orbis, Praque, Czechoslovakia. c. 1965

WADDELL, ROBERTA (Editor), *The Art Nouveau Style*, Dover Publications, Inc., New York. (1977)

WARREN, GEOFFREY, *All Color Book of Art Nouveau*, Octopus Books, Ltd., 59 Grosvenor St., London, W.1 (1972)

CATALOGUES

DOVER PUBLICATIONS, INC., The Crystal Palace Exhibition Illustrated Catalogue, London 1851, with new introduction by John Gloag, F.S.A.

FINCH COLLEGE MUSEUM OF ART, NY., Art Deco Catalog, Oct. 14-Nov. 30, 1970.

B. F. NORRIS, Alister & Co., 1893 Annual Catalogue, Chicago, Ill.

E. V. RODDIN & COMPANY, 1895 Catalogue, American Historical Catalog Collection, The Pyne Press, Princeton, New Jersey.

MERMOD & JACCARD JEWELRY CO. CATALOGUE, (Circa 1890), St. Louis, Missouri.

O & Y CO. CATALOGUE, 1913.

THE JEWELER'S CIRCULAR PUBLISHING CO., Trade Marks of The Jewelry and Kindred Trades.

THE NEW YORK JEWELER ILLUSTRATED ANNUAL CATALOG, S. F. M. Co., 1899.

MAGAZINES

COUNTRY LIFE IN AMERICA (May 1913)

HARPER'S BAZAAR (March 1900)

JEWELERS CIRCULAR WEEKLY (1913)

LADIES HOME COMPANION (1901, 1906)

LADIES HOME JOURNAL (June 1916)

THE DELINEATOR (February and March, 1900, July and October, 1901, November, 1902)

WOMAN'S HOME COMPANION, (September 1910)

SELECTED REFERENCE

Antiques and Collectibles – A Bibliography of Works in English, 16th Century to 1976, Linda Campbell Franklin, The Scarecrow Press, Inc., Metuchen, New Jersey. (1978)

Further research into exhibition catalogs and listed illustrated periodicals of the period will enable the reader to garner additional pertinent information about *Art Nouveau* and Art Deco jewelry.

ACKNOWLEDGEMENTS

My heartfelt thanks and gratitude to the following persons who graciously allowed their jewelry to be photographed:
Jenny Biddle/Cape Cottage Antiques
Mildred Combs
B. Halskov
Mike Iorg
Stan and Sylvia Katz/The Beautiful
  & The Unusual
Shelby Lewis
Papillion Antiques, (Sherman Oaks)
Martin Wolpert
Very special kudos to Mildred Combs and Jenny Biddle for their cooperation and assistance in ways too numerous to mention.

My appreciation to Connie Taylor for use of her office facilities and to Dena Archer for her assistance.

I'm much obliged to Lucile Nisen who assisted the author in the prodigious job of typing the manuscript.

My gratitude to Dave Hammell and to his wife, Barbara, who assisted him in the required tasks that consumed hours of dedication and hard work. His excellent photography is the result of Dave's infinite patience with the author as layouts were arranged and re-arranged. The superb color plates are the work of this award-winning cameraman and reflect his expertise in the handling of his equipment and his keen sense of lighting.

Praise must be given my husband who continues to tolerate the mysterious moods of an author-wife.

My appreciation to COLLECTOR BOOKS -- Bill and Meredith Schroeder --whose continued confidence in my work has made the publication of this book possible.

To all my readers who have written me urging me to write a book about the "new art" jewelry, my warmest thanks for your confidence and friendship without which this book could not have gained impetus nor completion.

The support and understanding of family and friends is immeasurable.